~ *les plus grands crus* ~

THE GREAT

WINES &

VINTAGES

This edition published by
CHARTWELL BOOKS, Inc.
A Division of BOOK SALES, Inc.
114 Northfield Avenue
Edison, New Jersey 08837
First English language edition, 1997
© Copyright, Paris, 1996

Photo engraving: SCAN 4

ISBN: 0-7858-0823-X

Printed in Spain

~les plus grands crus~

THE GREAT
WINES &
VINTAGES

DAVID COBBOLD

WITH HENRI GRANDCOLAS

PHOTOGRAPHY BY PHILIPPE HURLIN

CONTENTS

World map with geographical locations of all wines mentioned 6/7

AUTHOR'S NOTE

The selection of wines that constitute this book calls for a short explanation. The concept of "great wine" is complex and involves a wide variety of roles played by nature and also by man in dealing with what nature has provided. Many of these roles will be discussed in the following pages of this book, which aims to reveal aspects of the approach of those who make these wines. They share many points of view. And, fortunately for wine-lovers who enjoy the fascinating diversities of wine, there are differences between the outlooks of those who work on the same pieces of land as generations of their ancestors, and those who have created, from virtually nothing, wines considered by their peers as among the best in the world.

Every story has its beginning, and it often goes back further than is currently thought. For instance, one of the wines from the New World that figures in this book was considered as one of the world's greatest in the seventeenth century and has recently been revived. As the French poet Jean Cocteau said, tradition is a living thing.

The major constraint of selecting is having to eliminate options. I have many regrets about wines which deserve to be in this book but are not. What may be called the "classical" regions of fine wine production are well represented, which is justified by the fact that the modern concept of "great wine" was invented there. Other countries, from which an increasing number of great wines will emerge as time goes by, are also present, whereas countries such as Chile or Argentine are absent because, despite the considerable qualities of their wines, individual estates which regularly produce exceptional wines have yet to emerge there. The price factor has not been considered vital in determining the "greatness" of a wine. Great wines are usually expensive, when compared to merely good wines, due to the higher demand for a wine with a superior reputation. However the price of a wine does not determine its quality.

Two other criteria are important: that almost indefinable and therefore subjective notion of the aura of a wine, and that which a French agronomist once qualified as "a wine's honor," by which he meant a winemaker's dedication to producing the very best wine with nature has given. The spirit of permanent curiosity, of demanding the utmost at every stage, goes far beyond the search for profit.

My wish is that this book will provide the reader with a memorable journey around the widening world of fine wines.

40

39

41

42

13

24   25

8   9
3   7
2   5
4   6

31   30   29

Lebanon, the Bekaa Plain
1 Château Musar

France, Bordeaux
2 Château Margaux
3 Château Latour
4 Château Lafite-Rothschild
5 Château Mouton-Rothschild
6 Château Haut-Brion
7 Pétrus
8 Château Cheval Blanc
9 Château d'Yquem

France, Champagne
10 Bollinger
11 Roederer
12 Krug
13 Veuve Clicquot

France, Burgundy
14 La Romanée
15 La Romanée-Conti
16 Le Montrachet de Bouchard
   Père et Fils

France, Alsace
17 Domaine Weinbach
18 Zind-Humbrecht

France, Jura
19 Château d'Arlay

France, Côtes-du-Rhône
20 Château-Grillet
21 É. Guigal
22 Château de Beaucastel

France, Languedoc
23 Mas de Daumas Gassac

France, Loire
24 Domaine Huet
25 Coulée de Serrant

Italy, Tuscany
26 Sassicaia

Italy, Piedmont
27 Bruno Giacosa
28 Gaja

Spain, Castile-Leon
29 Bodegas Vega-Sicilia

Portugal, Porto
30 Taylor's Port
31 Quinta do Noval

Germany, Mosel-Saar-Ruwer
33 Johann Joseph Prüm
34 Maximin Grünhaus

Germany, Rheingau
35 Schloss Johannisberg
36 Weingut Robert Weil

Hungary, Tokay
37 Tokay

Austria, Burgenland
38 Rüster ausbruch

South Africa, Cape Province
39 Klein Constantia

United States, Napa Valley
40 Robert Mondavi and Opus One
41 Stag's Leap Wine Cellars

**United States,
Santa Cruz Mountains**
42 Ridge Vineyards

**Canada,
Niagara Peninsula**
43 Inniskillin Icewine

Australia
44 Penfold's Grange

**New Zealand,
Marlborough**
45 Cloudy Bay

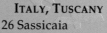

35 32
12 34
10 33
11
17
16 18
14
15
19
27
28
20
2 26
21
23
1
36
37
38
43
44

Château Musar

In 1930, Gaston Hochar founded Château Musar in Lebanon, adding another chapter to a tradition spanning several thousand years. In many ways, the wines of Musar sum up the history of wine in the world. Specialized historians generally agree that wine was first made about seven thousand years ago, somewhere in the part of the Near East which today covers the countries of Lebanon, Turkey, Georgia, and Syria. It is therefore logical to assume that the mildly scandalous behavior of Noah had something to do with a little overconsumption of the local wine.

In any event, although it may be difficult to locate the very first vineyards with any degree of precision, one thing seems certain: the ports of Byblos, Tyr, and Sidon were the first to trade in wine, thanks to the Phoenicians. Proof of this is to be found in writings on frescoes of tomb walls within Egyptian pyramids that go back six thousand years and mention the purple-hued wine from Mount Lebanon. It was the same Phoenicians, humanists and merchants, who propagated vine culture and wine-making all around the Mediterranean basin, from Greece to Italy and from Spain to France.

Visiting this country today is a deeply moving experience. The historical memory of this ancient crossroads between civilizations transpires through the courageous day-to-day efforts of its inhabitants to emerge from sixteen years of warfare. In Beirut, the battle scars of the war years are clearly visible on every street-corner. About twelve miles north of the capital, the cellars of Château Musar never closed throughout this unhappy period. Despite appalling conditions that would have deterred most people, the Hochar family continued to make wine. This is clearly a case where the particular strength of personality shown by this great wine can be linked to the tenacity of those who create it. Serge Hochar, who manages Musar with his brother, Ronald, never deserted Lebanon during those years of war, except for the occasional foray to spread the word of Musar around the wine-drinking world. During the worst of the shelling, he refused to modify his day's schedule and maintained his office, as well as the family apartment above the cellars, where he lived. Having placed his wife and children safely in Paris, he felt his place was at Musar. He had a special recipe for maintaining morale during the interminable hours of shelling: every day he would pour a bottle of a different vintage of Musar in a huge Baccarat glass and take one sip every hour. The shells could fall all around, but Serge Hochar was learning how Musar stood up to prolonged contact with air. The search for perfection can make a little local unrest seem so far away!

Thirty-five years of experience at Musar have not succeeded in destroying Hochar's natural modesty before the puzzling ways in which wine works. He continually experiments to try to resolve the mystery of wine's aging. Given that wine involves living matter, learning how it evolves is considered as vital by Serge

Opposite page: The Musar vineyards are situated in the Bekaa Valley of Lebanon, over 3,000 feet in altitude.
Above: Lebanon is at a crossroads between the oldest wine-growing civilizations, and many reminders are to be found, like this bas-relief with vine leaves from the Bacchus temple of Baalbek.

Hochar. This attitude is reflected in the unusually long time that Château Musar wines spend in the cellars before they are marketed: at least seven years. Could this be the age of reason? In many other respects, Serge Hochar refuses to submit to what have become standard procedures in modern wine-making. Blending incorporates wines from grape varieties which originate in different parts of France. For example, Cabernet Sauvignon from Bordeaux and Cinsault from the Rhone Valley are part of the blend in order to make a wine that will stand the test of time. If there were any doubts on that score, his 1970 red, or the extraordinary 1954 white made by his father, will quickly set them to rest. Tasting such wines brings to mind Rimbaud: "So, we have rediscovered eternity?" The very same vision of eternity is evoked by the earliest known text on wine, the epic of Gilgamesh,

written in Mesopotamia five thousand years ago: "I am searching for that disturbing complexity which has such extraordinary qualities; these wines are intensely alive and I search for the secret of eternal life through new blood. Man is in wine, and though I may hand down my secrets, nobody will ever make a wine like

mine." Serge Hochar is far too modest to use such words, but his everyday acts make them ring true.

The name Musar comes from the Arabic "m'zar," which means a remarkably beautiful place. Next to the current château building, which dates back to the eighteenth century, the winery and cellars

Above: Spring comes to the Château Musar cellars.
Right: Bottles of Musar age for at least seven years, the age of reason.
Opposite page: The war is over, hopefully, but it has left traces behind, even in Lebanon's vineyards.

delve down deep into the rocky hillside and harbor the considerable stocks made necessary by the aging policy and world demand.

The vineyards are about thirty miles inland from Château Musar in the Bekaa Valley at over 3,000 feet in altitude. The combination of this altitude and the surrounding mountains provides a surprisingly cool climate that can vary considerably from one vintage to another. Grape pickers come from Bedouin tribes that pass through the valley, which also harbors the temple of Bacchus at Baalbek. Even today, Lebanon is at the crossroads between East and West, ancient and modern. Those who taste Château Musar have the extraordinary opportunity of plugging into the history and diversity of the human spirit, which has always proved, even under adversity, its astonishing ability to innovate while using the fruit of experience.

Above: Musar's red wines age in cellars which were used as shelters during the war.

Right: Bacchus in his temple at Baalbek surveys the Musar vineyards.

Below: Arrak, with its unforgettable smell of aniseed, ages in amphoras, exactly as wine did at the time of the Romans or the Phoenicians.

TASTING NOTES

Château Musar's red wines share the fruity roundness of the Cinsault grape with the solid grip of the Cabernet Sauvignon. Such generalities are inadequate to account for their extraordinary complexity. The first vintage tasted is the one most recently on the market, the 1989.

◆ 1989

A fascinating nose that seems to oscillate between sharpness and softness. One seems to be about to identify a smell, and it fades away, only to reappear seconds later! This wine combines sensations of hot and cold, rather like cooking in the Middle Ages, which followed the alchemy principles of complementary elements. Initial warmth gives way to the freshness of fruit, with a

feeling of smoothness running through the wine's texture. The palate is alternately stimulated and caressed by multiple flavors.

◆ 1983

The nose is both rich and dense, reminding one of spiced jams. The wine is powerful in the mouth, as if the fruit had been concentrated and reduced through long, slow cooking. Below this is the fine texture typical of Musar, which will come through even stronger in a few years' time and will probably reach its peak in about twenty years.

◆ 1977

The wine is almost twenty years old, and it shows no sign of age. One can believe Serge Hochar when he says that he makes wines to last. The nose is between black currant and ink, as with some very young wines. The concentration of feelings on the palate makes it seem younger than the 1983. This combination of power and finesse is the perfect illustration of the paradox of Musar which, as it ages, shows alternately one, then another of its facets.

Château Margaux

Being the only classified growth of Bordeaux to bear the same name as its appellation gives Château Margaux a special status. Its name has not always been Margaux, however. The first references to the property date from 1750 and mention La Mothe, whose etymology resembles that of other famous Bordeaux growths, Lafite and Mouton, and describes the low ridges of higher ground formed here and there by the Gironde on its left bank in the Médoc area. Each of these hillocks rises over particularly deep layers of gravel and alluviums.

The future first growths, Margaux included, were first planted and developed by a small group of leading citizens of Bordeaux, most of whom were relatives. By the early eighteenth century, Margaux was firmly established as one of the leading properties making the deeper colored "French claret" of which every English gentleman had to have a barrel or two in his cellar. The fact that Margaux belonged to the same family as Haut-Brion for many years certainly helped to establish its reputation.

In these early days, the wines at Margaux were made by a remarkable man called Monsieur Berlon, who was the source of many innovations. A rapidly developing market for a new kind of wine created an unusual situation in the wine-making world and had several consequences. First of all, in order to supply the growing demand, new vineyards had to be planted, and the fresh plantings in the Médoc utilized the latest discoveries in the fields of viticulture and ampelography. The old practice of planting by "layering" the vines, which led to a dense mass of disorderly plants between which no horse-drawn instrument could pass, was

Left: The village church of Margaux used to be a private chapel to the Château when this was still called La Mothe.
Above: The central bands of barrels are deliberately stained with red wine to make a decoration out of the inevitable splashes that occur during filling and other activities.

Above: Built in 1811 by the architect Louis Combes, Margaux is the archetypal Bordeaux château.
Left: The interior, in this case the entrance hall, carries on the admirable classical style of the facade.
Below: The library.

abandoned. The new system of planting in rows made it far easier to look after the vines and harvest the grapes. In addition, progress was made in the selection of suitable grape varieties for the production of the type of wine required: deeply colored, strongly flavored, and able to age well. Cabernet sauvignon, which produces wines that fulfill all these requirements, rapidly emerged as the premier ingredient. Finally, Berlon

made red and white wines separately, an innovation at the time, and then incorporated roughly ten percent of white wine in the final blend. Perhaps this partly explains how Margaux acquired the reputation for being the most delicate of Bordeaux's first growths. Nowadays, white grapes on the property go to make the delicious Pavillon Blanc. Several generations later, Paul Pontallier, the current director of Margaux, is

carrying on the work of Monsieur Berlon. Born in the Sauternes area, he remembers his earliest personal experience of tasting a great wine as a memorable moment when, at the age of ten, he was allowed to put his lips to a glass of Yquem.
Like several of his colleagues, he readily admits that being confronted on a daily basis with exceptional wines does not necessarily provide the ideal viewpoint for an overall and objective vision of the

question of what does and what does not constitute a great wine. The name of a prestigious estate will evoke many things for a professional, as for an amateur, but how does one go about identifying the various components that constitute a great wine? Paul Pontallier has no hesitation in talking about the notion of absolutes in this context, as when certain wines impress one with a sensual feeling of depth. Harmony and balance are of the essence in such cases. As with painting or music, this way of looking at things requires a feeling for aesthetics. Although standards of beauty may vary as much for wine as they do in painting, Paul Pontallier is convinced that there are underlying rules which do not change, such as those that govern the notions of harmony and balance. The time factor is also extremely important in the case of a great wine, which can be very good in its youth, but will only develop its full potential after many years. To illustrate this, he says that the great vintages of Château Margaux are 1900, 1924, 1945, 1947, 1950, 1953, and 1961, and that since then, insufficient time has gone by for us to make a proper judgment on the more recent vintages!

Many other directors of Bordeaux's top châteaux agree with such a point of view, and wine critics would be well advised to pay more attention to this aspect of great wines. Charles Cocks, who wrote the first extensive guide to Bordeaux's wines in 1846, says precisely the same thing. In his book entitled *Bordeaux, Its Wines and the Claret Country*, he said, "A considerable period of time must go by before a final judgment can be pronounced on any vintage whatsoever."

Although our modern era involves haste in most fields, surely there is, for wine as for painting, a good case to be made for ever more patience. After all, the origin of the concept of a great wine has much to do with its capacity to age well and for a long time.

Tasting

Everybody agrees that the 1980's gave birth to a series of very fine vintages in Bordeaux. However, these wines will, in the case of the top châteaux, benefit from a further twenty or thirty years' cellaring, particularly in the case of Château Margaux, which probably has varied more, from one vintage to another, *than its fellow first growths. Only then, having gone beyond the stage of complexity that is part of any great wine, will Margaux attain that almost subliminal point, combining finesse and power, which is an ideal for a great Bordeaux wine. The potentially excellent vintages made at Margaux since 1982 are destined to become modern classics rich, smooth, and packed with flavor.*

Château Latour

It seems as if, for many centuries, the neighboring nations of France and England met either to fight wars or to do business, and sometimes to do both. During one such period, in 1351, the lords of Pauillac were granted the right to build a fortified tower. Six years later, the Plantagenets, who ruled over England, and the Valois, who governed France, started quarreling over the frontiers of their respective territories, bearing in mind that the English crown had inherited large parts of France, notably Aquitaine, which includes the Bordeaux area. This was the start of the Hundred Years' War between the two countries, which ended for England with the loss of its territories in France. During the process, the tower at Pauillac was destroyed. The ruins were rediscovered and the tower rebuilt in the seventeenth century, thus giving the initial name of "La Tour" to the property. The château itself is a relatively modest nineteenth-century bourgeois residence and cannot be seen from the road, unlike the tower which is the true symbol of Latour.

The extensive archives that have been preserved situate the beginnings of Latour as a wine estate in the early part of the eighteenth century. This was a period of strong demand, from the wealthy classes of Europe, for the new type of wine being produced in the future classified growths around Bordeaux. Later on, from 1863 to 1963, the estate remained the property of one family, and it was this period which developed Latour's reputation. Subsequently, after belonging to a British company for a number of years, Latour was acquired by a French group in 1993. When, in 1855, a large number of Bordeaux châteaux were classified into five different levels, Latour was ranked, together with three others, at the top level of first growth. On its label which proudly shows this classification, Latour adds, in capital

Above: Vines derive considerable benefits from these gravel soils, known as "graves."
Right: A distinction won at the World's Fair in Paris in 1900.
Below: The dining room in the château.

Above: The tower that supplies the estate with its name, its landmark and its emblem.

struck by large expanses of vines on essentially flat land which, from time to time, undulates slightly. What explains the fact that such vineyards produce such a large number of wines considered as part of the world's best? One of the main reasons is that there are excellent drainage conditions here. The Médoc soil has been built up by sedimentary deposits carried down by the Garonne River from its source in the Pyrenees mountains. These contain high proportions of gravels, of various diameters, which have been deposited in layers on the left bank of the Gironde estuary. In the Pauillac area, these gravels, mixed with clay, are twelve feet deep, and are particularly stony on the Latour estate. This situation provides ideal natural drainage, as well as a secondary benefit of reflecting the sunlight and heat upwards to the ripening bunches of grapes. Furthermore, the local climate is ideal for the production of fine wine, as the sunshine period is well distributed during the growing season, and the nearby Atlantic Ocean tempers excessive temperatures, whether hot or cold, which could damage grapes or vines.

At Latour, although the specific geology is considered important, it is the balance between climate and soil factors that is given the main role. A blend of these elements produces what the French call "terroir," which refers to the specific natural environment that makes each wine unique. The directors at Château Latour believe that progress in wine-making techniques made over the past couple of decades has largely contributed to making wines more drinkable in their youth. Putting wine on a pedestal may make it admired, but doing so removes it from the realm of pleasure. Prestige and usage must find a proper balance, in wine as in other fields. The role of man is to reveal the potential that lies hidden in the raw material, and current vintages of Château Latour may not require twenty years' cellaring before they can be enjoyed.

letters, the words "Grand Vin," to distinguish the best wine of the property from others, like the excellent "Forts de Latour" that may be produced on the estate. As for its style, which has been particularly distinctive over the years, it is definitely a wine built to last and can be fairly austere in its youth. As it ages, it acquires incredible finesse. All wines evolve, necessarily, but surely the new owners will maintain the essence of the rich heritage of Latour.

The estate overlooks the Gironde estuary and spreads around the château. It has often been said that fine wines come from poor soil. In most cases around the world, such soils are linked to hillside vineyard sites. Erosion has thinned the layer of top soil, thus impoverishing it, and the slope provides the natural drainage required by the vine. But here in the Médoc, as in the Graves area, there are no hills and one is

Château Lafite-Rothschild

What was the Médoc area like in the sixteenth century? A little-trodden wilderness, filled with marshes and sheep grazing also renowned for its good hunting grounds and wicked bandits. Nobody mention of wine, which at the time was produced elsewhere, generally closer to Bordeaux or much further upstream in what was known as the upper country, in places like Gaillac, Cahors, or Bergerac, whose wines supplied up to half the volume of what was, at that time, sold as Bordeaux. A few vineyards existed in the Médoc, but these produced wines solely for local consumption. In 1572, the estate of Lafite was divided into no less than sixty farms of which wheat was the principal crop. It is very hard for today's visitor to the Médoc to imagine such a landscape, as vineyards seem to dominate the scene and give the impression of always having been there, surrounding the many large châteaux which often appear as proof of centuries-old traditions. But, in fact, these châteaux were nearly all built during the eighteenth and nineteenth centuries, during which period the Médoc caught up and overtook all other Bordeaux areas as the prime producer of its top wines. The surge in demand for a particular style of red wine, emanating largely from markets in northern parts of Europe, encouraged members of the Bordeaux parliament and other worthy citizens to rush to purchase land in the Médoc, which was then rapidly planted to vineyards. This sudden craze was amply commented upon at the time, as contemporary texts speak of "planting fever."

The fact that the first vineyard plots to be planted during this period were to become, a century later, "first growths" under the 1855 classification is not merely fortuitous. The early investors knew exactly what they were looking for in the Médoc: deep layers of gravel, or "graves," which would enable them to reproduce conditions as close as possible to those at Haut-Brion, which had created a market for similar wines. The first and most noteworthy of these pioneers was Nicolas-Alexandre, marquis of Ségur. Nobody in the Bordeaux area ever equaled his influence. President of the Bordeaux parliament during the first part of the eighteenth century, he was simultaneously owner of Lafite, Latour, and Mouton, as well as Calon-Ségur and countless lesser properties. His elegance was legendary, and the buttons of his dress coat shone so brightly that Louis XV was intrigued by them. The king was surprised to learn that, far from diamonds, they were made from highly polished stones, picked from his vineyards. Ségur escaped the fate of Fouquet, whose power and wealth were considered by the monarch to have attained dangerous proportions, but he did earn the unofficial title of "Prince of the Vineyards." Ségur was the first to separate the estates of Mouton and Lafite, which opened the way for the creation of two distinct styles of wines.

Once the treaties of Utrecht were signed, Franco-British relations could turn from warfare to commerce, which had hardly been abandoned, although most of it was illegal. While the barrels of the

Opposite page: Château Lafite was one of the first wine-growing estates to be planted in the Médoc, at the turn of the seventeenth and eighteenth centuries.
Above: The living rooms show the influence of the late nineteenth century, when James de Rothschild acquired Lafite.

Above: The pink and purple hues of the winery buildings remind one of wine.
Left: The new underground barrel cellar, designed by the architect Ricardo Bofil.
Below: The green drawing room.

guns cooled down, barrels of wine started rolling. The first written traces of Château Lafite date from these years between 1715 and 1720. In 1719, Lord Bristol managed to procure a considerable quantity of French wines, including some "La Fite claret," without having to disguise it as being of some other origin, which was the strategy of British claret lovers during the war years. Even the prime minister, Sir Robert Walpole, brought in barrels of Lafite to his cellar at Houghton Hall, declaring the wine to be Portuguese! After all, how can one rob oneself? This lesson in the subtleties of government and the use of position was not to be lost on a future owner of Haut-Brion. Monsieur de Talleyrand, during the difficult years of the French revolution and the Napoleonic era, always considered that nations could be governed without abnegating one's own interests. Beyond such anecdotes of personal interest, it is easy to understand that statistics on the destination of French wines during these periods are to be taken with a pinch of salt.

The Lafite collection of old vintages form an extraordinary data bank of the history of the property. The only missing vintage is that of 1793, for the simple reason that, during the French revolution the then-owner, Pichard, was unable to deal with the harvest, as he was condemned by the authorities, the guillotine had replaced the pruning knife. Afterwards, and despite the commercial and manpower problems caused by Napoleon's war-mongering, Lafite prospered and managed to sell for prices considerably higher than those of its most illustrious direct competitors. For example, the 1844 vintage sold for 4 500 francs per barrel, which was more than double the price obtained by Margaux or Latour. Eleven years before the famous classification of 1855 which sealed, for a considerable period of time, the hierarchy of Médoc properties, this vintage put Lafite in an unbeatable position to obtain the highest rank. This classification was based on the average prices obtained by each wine over a given number of years. Lafite came out first of the first growths.

Today, Lafite maintains its status as a mythical and somewhat mysterious wine. The Baron Eric de Rothschild lives in the château, which his family bought in 1868. Those who wish to visit require patience, as they must comply with a complicated ritual that involves obtaining an appointment via an office in Paris, which in many cases will only be scheduled for a date six months later. The former stewards of the estate

now have the title of Technical Director, but the job is the same and is of vital importance to the well-being of the property. One of the most famous stewards at Lafite was Joseph Goudal, during the nineteenth century. His successor today, Monsieur Chevalier, is, like many of his colleagues, the son of a wine-grower. In his opinion, making a fine wine requires an accumulation of experience that can only be acquired through a vast number of contacts, exchanges of ideas, tests, and comparisons, which all add up to a sort of reference grid that enables the wine-maker to guide himself in the decisions he has to make.

A great wine is recognized, at first sight, by its label, when it is well-known. This is a sort of standard-bearer that carries with it all the legends and history that have helped awaken the imagination of the wine-lover. But a wine can only be truly judged in the glass, according to Monsieur Chevalier. What follows is an individual's appreciation of the infinite variety of styles and sensations that make wine such a fascinating subject matter.

TASTING

The capacity of a wine to stimulate conversation is probably one of the signs of its greatness. Naturally, the occasion at which a wine has been tasted will influence judgments, but subjective elements are a necessary part of the appreciation of a wine.

One may prefer a wine in its youth, for the sensual pleasure of tasting something not too far removed from fresh grapes. As time goes by, one's preference may go to wines which have sublimated their primary flavors into a balance between these and the essence of their "terroir." This is where truly great wines show themselves. In the case of Lafite, it takes maybe fifteen years for the wine to release its full potential of aromas with an incredibly silky texture.

Château Mouton-Rothschild

Pomp and circumstance are words that spring to the visitor's mind when arriving at the Mouton-Rothschild estate. Everything here is beautiful and manicured: stately buildings harmoniously blend into the green parkland and gardens, and a crowning touch of majesty is lent by the splendid trees which stand all around. It is more than probable that aesthetics presided over the conception of the estate in its current form, and the result is conclusive: Mouton-Rothschild is a work of art. Once again the thesis of that great historian of wine, Roger Dion, is confirmed— namely, that it is impossible to understand the geographical situations of France's vineyards without taking into account the will of man. The Rothschild saga is very much present at Mouton. When he took charge of the property in 1922, Baron Philippe de Rothschild inherited a Mouton classified as a second growth of Pauillac, in the Médoc. Considering this rank insufficient, the Baron made every effort to improve it. Much has been said and written about this famous classification of 1855, which seemed, and indeed still seems, to be unchangeable. What is it? In order to clarify the diversity of the various Bordeaux Châteaux wines that were to be displayed at the Universal Exhibition held in Paris in 1855, their owners decided to establish a classification system. They entrusted this delicate task to the "courtiers," or wine-brokers, whose expertise could not be questioned. How were they to judge each wine relative to its competitors? To evaluate the

Left: 30,000 visitors come to Mouton annually, above all for the wine, but also for the calm beauty of the park and gardens. Above: The hand of man has imposed a style here.

production of a wine estate merely on the evidence of a single one of its wines, tasted on a given day, would have removed that essential factor of a wine's quality: its ability to stand the test of time. It would be rather like trying to judge a film by a still photograph of one of its scenes. The courtiers therefore decided that the market was the best judge of a wine's relative value, provided that the statistics were taken over a reasonable number of years. They therefore weighed the market prices obtained by each wine that was submitted, over a period of about a hundred years. The average price obtained by each wine over the period determined its ranking within one of five categories, the most expensive being classified "first growths," and so on. The only problem with this system, which was certainly the best when it was devised, is

Above: During the crucial period of fermentation, one cellar-master at Mouton preferred to sleep beside his vats to hear them chattering during the night, rather than go home to his bed.
Below: The gardens at sunrise.

that it has never subsequently taken into account the changes in the relative merits of the wines, with the notable exception of Mouton-Rothschild. Clearly if it was done again today, there would be considerable changes.

Having battled for years to have Mouton-Rothschild promoted, Baron Philippe de Rothschild was finally rewarded by its being classified, by official decree, first growth in 1973. Nobody has ever seriously disputed this ranking since. Philippe de Rothschild was a remarkable man and broke new ground in a number of fields. He was the first château owner in Bordeaux to insist on all his wine being bottled at the château, whereas his colleagues continued, for a while, the tradition of selling their wine in barrels to wine-merchants. He also innovated by asking artists to illustrate the labels of Mouton. For the 1924 vintage, he commissioned a design from the contemporary designer Jean Carlu. This was considered much too avant-garde at the time by the majority of Mouton-Rothschild's customers, and the idea was not renewed until 1945, when, to celebrate the Allied victory in the Second World War, it was revived, never to be abandoned again. Every vintage of Mouton since then has borne a different label, each one signed by a well-known artist. Several other wine estates were to use the idea later on, but it must be said that Baron Philippe was the initiator of this highly symbolic link between fine wine and the world of art. As to those who have provided designs for the labels of the successive vintages, their names constitute a fabulous catalogue of modern art: Picasso, Bacon, Cocteau, Braque, Dalí, Moore, Alechinsky, Miró, Kandinsky, Motherwell, Warhol, and Balthus are just a few examples. And to confirm his love of art and beautiful objects, Baron Philippe created a museum in the château, where the thirty thousand annual visitors can admire an extraordinary collection centered on the theme of wine in art.
Following in her father's footsteps, Philippine de Rothschild now presides over the destiny of the estate. She also believes that wine and art are inseparable, as both demand a solid culture in their respective fields in order to be appreciated. She is fascinated by the devotion to the land and wine of Mouton that is shown by the team that makes the wine. The reward of such teamwork was visible on the cellar-master's face when he saw the first wine of the 1995 vintage

being run out of a fermenting vat; such depth of color and intensity of perfumes engendered instant enthusiasm. The very notion of a great wine is always relative, even for those who make such wines. A long experience of the wines from a given estate, together with those of all the competitors which a cellar-master will inevitably taste, serves to raise the level of expectancy. This can be read in the remark of Philippe Cottin, director of Mouton, who says that it is impossible to make a "great" Mouton every year: the laws of nature and good fortune, always unpredictable, make sure that monotony will never set in. Monsieur Cottin considers that the current vision of great wines initially emerged in the 1950's and has led to an almost intangible concept, linked to a large extent to the means that were then available to producers and to criteria specific to a small number of buyers. A great wine is necessarily a wine that surpasses itself. What complicates judgment is time's perspective at least a generation is required to truly estimate the excellence of a wine.

TASTING

◆ *Mouton-Rothschild 1994*
The nose reminds one of concentrated, dark-colored fruit. The mouth feeling is full, smooth, and long-lasting. The final note is one of freshness, which gives good overall balance.

◆ *Mouton-Rothschild 1990*
The nose is still very fresh and young, with smells of red and black berry fruit. As it opens out in the glass, through contact with the air, more complex aromas start to come through. The mouth shows a combination of richness and austerity, and the overall impression is that of reined-in power with elegance.

Château Haut-Brion

Wine is a product of circumstances, linked both to a place and to a moment, and is subject to contemporary taste, which is linked to both individual preference and surrounding culture. When a wine's reputation is lasting, its name becomes part of a cultural entity, but it remains essentially dependent on individual taste, which evolves with time. Nobody can describe the taste of wine during Roman times, but specialists are in agreement that it was very different from that of wine today. The same can be said of the wines of Bordeaux, which have changed considerably since the Middle Ages. Over the centuries, production techniques and ways of keeping wine have combined to form new tastes, which, in turn, form consumers who expect different styles. For instance, up to the seventeenth century, Bordeaux produced more white or pale red (the wine the English initially called "claret") wines than red. The famous British author Samuel Pepys wrote in his diary; "I tasted a French wine called Ho-Bryan, which was of good taste, the most unusual I have ever encountered." This is the first written evidence of a new style of Bordeaux wine and of the role that a few large estates were to play in the creation of what was to become, in the nineteenth century, the Grand Cru classification system. Pepys' diary, despite his uncertain spelling, is also evidence that Haut-Brion was the very first of these new estates.

Left: A residence worthy of one of its most illustrious former owners, Talleyrand, who never in fact lived here.
Above: The only estate of the Graves area to be classified as first growth in 1855, together with three châteaux from the Médoc, which were later joined by fourth.

At the time when Samuel Pepys was tasting his first glass of Haut-Brion, Arnaud de Pontac was the owner. His great grandfather had built the château, just south of the town of Bordeaux on some poor land known as "graves" on account of the high proportion of sand and gravel that the soil contained. Such land was going to prove, in Bordeaux as elsewhere, that the best wines generally come from the poorest soils. Apart from this technical aspect, Arnaud de Pontac had fully realized that the best could be sold for the most, and he therefore invested considerably in order to improve his wine's quality.

Since that time, several owners, many of them famous, have possessed Château Haut-Brion. One of them was Talleyrand, who bought it in 1801 at the time when he was Napoleon's Minister for External Affairs. History does not reveal whether one of the motivations behind his purchase might have been the supply of wine for Mass, as many years had gone by since the former bishop had ceased to perform religious duties. Much later, in 1935, the estate was acquired by Clarence Dillon, a New York financier, who maintained those investments vital to an estate of this kind during a period of severe economic crisis. More recently, in 1961, Haut-Brion was a pioneer among the hitherto highly traditional Bordeaux wineries by installing stainless steel tanks for fermenting the wine. Nearly all the châteaux have since abandoned the old wooden vats for this practice. Haut-Brion used to stand in the country, but now has been encircled by the urban sprawl of modern Bordeaux. It is the only wine from the Graves area to be classified on a par with the other first growths from the Médoc: Lafite, Latour, Margaux, and Mouton. It falls under the recently created Pessac-Leognan appellation, which, as the northern part of Graves, responds to that curious French mania for constantly subdividing their already overcomplicated appellation systems into ever smaller slices of land.

Above: Haut-Brion is the oldest established of the Grands Crus of Bordeaux and used to be beyond the city limits. Today, both the château and the vineyards are surrounded by urban development, which makes Haut-Brion the most urban of the world's great wine estates. Despite the limited space that this implies, Jean-Bernard Delmas, the director, has put together a fascinating collection of different varieties of vine plants, which makes Haut-Brion a natural reserve for wine-lovers in several respects.

Above: The château's reserve cellar contains an impressive series of old vintages.
Below: Some of Haut-Brion's famous former owners. From left to right: Arnaud de Pontac, Charles-Maurice de Talleyrand-Périgord, and Clarence Dillon.

Haut-Brion harbors a wonderful ampelographic museum whose rich collection of varieties of vitis vinifera is proof of the extraordinary plant diversity behind wine production. Monsieur Delmas, the director of Haut-Brion, explains that the notion of a great wine implies a juxtaposition of several elements: specific site, weather conditions, and time. To be able to say that a wine will be great requires a considerable number of tastings, held at different stages and under different circumstances. Nature is variable by definition, and this has to be taken into consideration. The exceptional cannot be standardized, so there is no use hoping that a great wine will be made every year. Favorable circumstances, involving both soil, plant-life, and climate, are required for an ideal state of ripeness to be obtained in the grapes. It is the wine-grower's job to decide if and when that moment has come, and, from then on, all the technical equipment in the world can only help reveal a natural potential.

Pétrus

If you were driving around the Pomerol area, searching for the estate that produces the most expensive wine from Bordeaux, the mythical Château Pétrus, what would you expect to see? Probably a splendid, grandiose château, surrounded by impressive grounds. The reality is rather different, as when you finally find the place, usually with some difficulty, Pétrus' buildings are in fact a modest house, with a neighboring barn in the classic style of the area. This establishment is unusual among the top estates of Bordeaux, where great wines often go with grand houses, but Pétrus is on the right bank of the Dordogne River, far from the grandeur of the Médoc estates which stretch along the left bank of the Gironde estuary. It is here, in this northern part of the Bordeaux area, that two of the most prestigious appellations of Bordeaux are to be found: St. Emilion and Pomerol. The estates of Pomerol are, for the most part, both younger and smaller in vineyard size than those of St. Emilion. They only came to fame quite recently, as the worldwide reputation of Pétrus as a top estate goes back to the 1960's at the earliest, and its undisputed status as the equivalent of a first growth among the unclassified estates of Pomerol is even more recent.

One of the outside walls of what we must, for want of a better word, call the château, harbors a statue of St. Peter, whose Latin name, *Petrus,* has been bequeathed on the château, although nobody seems to know why. The small size of the property and the apparent modesty of the buildings makes one curious about the meteoric rise to greatness of this estate. Nowadays it has added the paradox of being inaccessible in terms of price and more forward, and therefore more accessible, in terms of taste than most other great wines from Bordeaux.

Above: The vineyard at Pétrus covers a mere thirty acres. Opposite (upper): The statue of St. Peter, whose Latin name is that of the estate. Opposite (lower): The monastic simplicity of the tanks at Pétrus.

Grown on cool, clay-rich soils, it manages to appear fresh and almost tender on the palate. The vineyard site, on the crest of a plateau in the center of Pomerol, gives it advantages in terms of improved drainage and depths of soil, but this is insufficient to explain the wine's qualities, as it is hard to talk about a specific "terroir," notably different from its immediate neighbors, in the case of Pétrus. A look into the winery reveals none of the trappings of modern wine-making technology. A couple of rows of small concrete vats and a modest number of wooden barrels are all that is required. What is the secret of Pétrus? It comes back, once again, to the necessity of taking into consideration the will of man in the making of a great wine. In the case of Pétrus, it was a woman who determinedly raised it to its rank of the greatest among Pomerols. Madame Loubat, the former owner of Pétrus, could never understand why the first growths

Above: Merlot is the almost exclusive grape variety at Pétrus. In these barrels it can show its paces sooner than the other leading variety in Bordeaux, the Cabernet Sauvignon.

first, scarcity second, and, with a little help from a few American critics, Pétrus became the most desirable, and expensive, wine in Bordeaux.

For its current owners, Pétrus is less cerebral than the Médoc growths, and therefore easier to like. Its style is described as baroque, which can be attributed to its composition, using, almost exclusively, the Merlot grape. But Pétrus, like other wines built to last, can be austere in its youth on account of its extreme concentration.

of the Médoc fetched higher prices than the wine of her estate. She decided to do everything in her power to reverse the situation. A few decades later, Pétrus has definitely acquired mythic status. Quality

TASTING

◆ *Pétrus 1994*

Tasting wines of this level when they are still very young can be difficult. They really should be kept for a further five or ten years at least. Color, in a young wine of this type, is always very dense. The nose is fresh and elegant, with fruit aromas that are as clear as a bell. The first sensation in the mouth is of depth and fullness. Its youth shows through a certain lightly knit austerity.

Château Cheval Blanc

Cheval Blanc means "white horse" in French, and the famous château of St. Emilion is as much an exception as is its namesake in equine terms. Its history is relatively short for a Bordeaux château, as it was founded on the right-hand bank of the Dordogne River less than two centuries ago. Until 1832, the vineyards that currently make up the estate of Cheval Blanc were just a part of Château Figeac, which then sold thirty seven acres of vines to the Fourcaud-Lussac family. Since then, the estate has rapidly acquired one of the finest reputations in St. Emilion and has gradually increased in size to ninety one acres today. This size may seem relatively modest compared to the extensive Médoc estates, which are frequently double the size, but it is quite large for the right bank area. St. Emilion waited until 1955, a century later than Médoc, to classify its wines, but has subsequently revised this classification twice, in 1985 and again in 1996. On each occasion, Cheval Blanc has won the race, neck and neck with Ausone, each being given the highest possible ranking of Premier Cru Classé "A." Cheval Blanc has never changed hands and still belongs to the family who originally founded it. In all probability, this continuity has helped it to acquire its reputation, as the family is directly involved with the estate and has always done everything to maintain standards. In fact, Cheval Blanc is the only one of Bordeaux's top estates never to have changed ownership.

The house is classical in style and harmoniously set with its winery buildings in a magnificent park, and there is even a private chapel next to the château. Impeccably aligned rows of vines guard the buildings on all sides. Cheval Blanc is situated in that part of St. Emilion which borders on Pomerol, and its soil types are extremely variable, including limestone, marl, and clay over limestone. One of the other unusual features of the estate is the proportion of grape varieties used in its wines. There is no sign of any Cabernet Sauvignon, and the dominant variety is, unusually, Cabernet Franc. Merlot, the king of Pomerol, and a touch of Malbec complete the blend.

Whatever the ingredients used to make the wine, the results are impressive: wines of extreme delicacy which, in their youth, frequently disappoint those who seek power above subtlety. But these wines are good at any point of their life, which is admirably long. Although it is notoriously difficult to attribute a wine's character to a single element in its composition, it is fairly safe to wager that the extreme finesse of Cheval Blanc stems from the intricate combination between many different types of soil and its particular balance of grape varieties. A good example of Cheval Blanc's capacity to attain finesse and balance is the 1975 vintage. So many Bordeaux wines of this year have turned out overly hard and unyielding, whereas Cheval Blanc is a model of perfectly smooth, elegant harmony in its flavors.

Since 1991, Pierre Lurton has been the managing director of Cheval Blanc. He comes from one of Bordeaux's great wine

Opposite page: The vineyards spread around the château, over widely diversified soils.
Above: The house is harmoniously classic in its facade.

families, and a very extensive one at that. His opinion is that "terroir" is the true basis for all classification of wines. Indeed, it is very hard not to be struck by the impact of particular ecosystems that will enable grapes to ripen earlier on specific vineyard plots than on those nearby, thus reducing the risk from damage due to late season storms. As for the part played by human beings in the making of great wines, Pierre Lurton quotes the great enologist Emile Peynaud, who once said that great wines were made despite man's interventions.

This modesty in the face of nature and her mysteries is frequently found in those who make such wines. Taking a back seat to what nature has provided, man simply tries to foresee as best he can and guides the more or less natural course of events. It follows from this that a great wine is essentially produced in the vineyards and that the role of the wine-grower is of greater importance than that of the enologist. His job is to estimate the potential of a given patch of soil and its vines, so that year after year he will be able to predict which plots will produce the best fruit. When everything is ready, the wine-maker's job is then to nurse along wines in the making in the most unobtrusive way possible. He cannot do this job well unless there is perfect

teamwork between those in charge of the vineyard and those in the winery. Once the fermentation is finished, the wine has to be raised until it is ready to be bottled. As with most of Bordeaux's greatest wines, Cheval Blanc ages in new oak barrels, for a length of time that varies according to the wine's characteristics. This very natural method of aging enables the wine to gradually clarify itself through gravity, thus avoiding the necessity for filtering which could remove some of its substance, and thus flavor.

When he talks about the subject of great wines, Pierre Lurton uses a wide range of striking analogies drawn from everyday life, preferring such comparisons to either complicated technical terms or precious frills. The main quality of a wine for him is how easy it is to taste and drink. He wonders how much pleasure is derived from the drinking of extremely bitter coffee, for example, and concludes that a wine should, at all times, be pleasurable to the drinker. When the discussion turns to a wine's capacity to stand the test of time, he talks about wool clothing, and wonders whether a stiffly thick island sweater is actually warmer than a fine and supple cashmere, and which will actually last the longest? Naturally, being able to judge whether or not a wine is great requires some firsthand experience and a bit of training, rather like driving a formula one race car, but pleasure should always be spontaneous. With its incomparable finesse, Cheval Blanc certainly fulfills that requisite.

TASTING

◆ *The good vintages*
Cheval Blanc has produced some legendary vintages, like 1921, 1934, 1947 (one of the most sought after Bordeaux of all time), 1949, 1952, 1955, 1964, 1966, 1970, 1978, 1982, 1983, and 1990. And let's not forget the 1975, which is about the best wine in Bordeaux from that vintage.

Opposite page: The private chapel of Cheval Blanc. Just imagine what the communion wine would taste like! Above: The park surrounds the château, the chapel, and the winery buildings. Below: A family that has never ceased to play an important part in running the estate.

Château d'Yquem

Of Bordeaux's many prestigious châteaux, Yquem is the only one that possesses a true medieval castle building. This is proof enough that the French word for château describes a fine house rather than a fortress. Built in the twelfth century on the highest part of Sauternes, Yquem overlooks the Garonne Valley to the southwest of Bordeaux. Although the building that carries the name of Yquem is the oldest of Bordeaux's châteaux, its wine has been renowned for a considerably shorter time, as its celebrity dates from the nineteenth century. This impressive building shows traces of the region's history, after being built by the English during their three hundred year presence in Aquitaine. The name Yquem is similar to that of the patronymic name of the sixteenth-century philosopher from the region, Michel Eyquem de Montaigne, better known as Montaigne. Is there any link between the two names? Probably not, although the root of both words, originally German, is "aig-helm" which comes from "aigan," meaning "to have," and "helm," meaning "helmet." The château was acquired in 1592 by the family Sauvage d'Yquem, whose last direct descendant, Françoise-Josephine, married Count Louis-Amedée de Lur-Saluces in 1785. One of the direct descendants of this marriage, Count Alexandre de Lur-Saluces, is the current director of the estate. The example of Yquem perfectly illustrates the principles of continuity and perseverance, so vital to the creation and lasting quality of a great wine. The capacity and greatness of a bottle of Yquem can easily be measured in generations rather than merely in years.

Opposite: Yquem is the only medieval château building among the first growths of Bordeaux.
Above: The cellar collection at Yquem includes vintages from the eighteenth and nineteenth centuries.

Topographic situations can often help one to grasp the nature of the ingredients that go to make a great wine. What strikes one immediately at Yquem is the subtle contrast between the extreme softness of the landscape and the relative austerity of the buildings, slightly mellowed by the ebb and flow of the years. Like a rock in the midst of an ocean of vines, which appear golden and silky in the pale autumn sunlight, Château Yquem stands upright over the folds of land that roll towards the Garonne River. Driving into the estate early in the morning with mist rising from the valley, one can feel that there is something special in the air. These morning mists just before harvest time are extremely important for a property like Yquem.

They provoke the formation of a special form of fungus, known as "noble rot," which concentrates sugar in the grapes. Under other circumstances, wine-growers

Above: The banner of the de Saluces regiment.
Opposite: Yquem's vineyard is kept like a garden, and the earth is heeled up over the vine stalks to protect them during the winter months.
Below: The château's interior shows the patina of centuries of history. It has a special blend of majesty and country simplicity.

Yquem at table

An older vintage of Yquem should be drunk by itself, without food. Vintages from the past twenty years can be tried with foie gras, or, better still, with roquefort, a blue-veined cheese made with sheep's milk.

would do everything possible to avoid their grapes becoming rotten, but for the production of the greatest sweet wines, this fungus is a precious ally when it happens at the right moment. It is provoked by a tiny mushroom called botrytis cinerea, a shrinks the grape's skin, without causing it to burst open. This makes for a rapid increase of sugar, acid, and other flavor ingredients, relative to the volume of juice in each grape. The mushroom grows only under specific weather conditions which combine high humidity levels in the early mornings followed by warm sunny days. Such local climatic phenomena occur in those rare parts of the world that are able, in certain years, to produce very rich sweet wines: the Mosel and Rhine valleys in Germany, Tokay in Hungary, Rust in Austria, Alsace, parts of the Loire Valley, and, of course, the Sauternes area.

Know-how is an essential part of ensuring the success any great wine, but it will never ensure that such a wine will continue to exist. Unless the wine finds a market that is prepared to pay for it, it will cease to exist. Yquem was fortunate enough to have customers like George Washington, who ordered 360 bottles for his personal cellar in the early days. Its reputation thus assured by famous customers, wine-lovers from Russia and the United States, from France and Japan, from Holland and Germany followed suit over the next two centuries, ready to spend a couple of hundred dollars per bottle.

Count Lur-Saluces considers that to taste a great wine, one must be prepared for discovery and then concentrate fully in order to weigh up one's sensations. Sometimes a special sort of dialogue will establish itself between the taster and the wine. In most cases, there remains a large share of mystery, as it is impossible to reduce a great wine to a purely technical explanation. Technical details obviously have their place, but their importance is limited to an amateur. The production of great wines is above all a human creation, maybe even humanistic. The team that works at Yquem is a living example of devotion to a cause, and Alexandre de Lur-Saluces pays homage to them in saying: "Our people make the wine here, just as much as the sun or the soil."

Only the women pick the grapes at Yquem, as this kind of harvest requires extreme patience and dexterity. The price of excellence has almost no limits, and there have been years when no Yquem was sold, such as 1910, 1952, 1964, or 1974.

Bollinger

Champagne is the northernmost vineyard in France. This geographical condition has been instrumental in the emergence of two techniques that are characteristic of wine-making in Champagne and which have been developed to a fine art in this area: blending wines from different vineyards and a secondary fermentation carried out in bottles. This latter phenomenon probably started by accident, but was progressively understood and gradually mastered, having been initially stimulated by the interest in sparkling wines shown by some English consumers in the seventeenth century. A cool climate like that of Champagne produces naturally light and delicate wines, low in alcohol. Such wines form an ideal basis for making sparkling wines. As for blending, made necessary in Champagne by the unequal maturity levels of grapes from different vineyards and from one year to another, it is fair to say that wine-makers in Champagne have managed to transform a handicap into an advantage. Three grape varieties are used: Pinot Noir, Pinot Meunier, and Chardonnay. The diversity of soils, of slopes, and of sun angle that prevail in the Champagne vineyards multiply the palette of tastes available to the blender. Thus every Champagne producer, or "house" as they are often called, has gradually developed a particular style of wine, according to the objectives, the tastes and the raw materials available to him. "House style" is thus the main factor that marks the difference between one Champagne and another.

Without a doubt, Bollinger's style is particularly distinctive and stems from a series of clear choices made and then patiently applied by the successive directors of this family-owned house. Bollinger considers that the house should be judged not on the strength of one of their rarer wines, produced in limited quantities, but on their non-vintage wine, which constitutes the vast majority of their production. But each wine in the range has

Traditional marker in the Champagne vineyard indicating one of Bollinger's plots.

Above: Bollinger's attractive house in the village of Aÿ.
Left: This cellar is the resting place for the wine its fans refer to as "RD," for "recently disgorged." It will stay here for about ten years.

dedication necessary to the production of a wine—from the beginnings in the vineyard, through all the steps of making and aging, until it is delivered to the customer, with the sole objective of quality based on integrity. In such a process, the guiding factor is a rigorous approach that excludes any short-term profit-seeking. It is clear that the greatest wines cannot emerge otherwise, even if some of them manage to repay their owner's long-term investment quite well later on.

The RD is proof of Bollinger's will to pursue a specific aim while paying tribute to a traditional practice in Champagne. Anyone needing proof that good champagne can age extremely well can turn to the RD, which has been aged for at least ten years in Bollinger's cellars before being disgorged and marketed, whereas the majority of vintage champagne that is shipped and sold is between four and six years old. The idea is that longer aging of the wine in ideal cellar conditions and in contact with the yeasts that have achieved the secondary fermentation will give additional dimensions to the flavor and enable it to last longer.

The Vieilles Vignes Françaises is a unique case in Champagne, and something extremely rare in Europe, of a wine made from ungrafted vines, densely planted and trained on posts as they used to be in most vineyards up to the late nineteenth century. This method of culture implied renewing vine plants by "layering" a young vine shoot under the soil and pinning it there until it rooted and produced a new plant, which could be severed from its parent. One of the disadvantages of this system was that the vineyard soon resembled a jungle into which it was impossible to go with a horse to plow, for instance. All work had to be done by hand, and the vineyard plots rapidly comprised plants of varying ages

and yields. The arrival of phylloxera was to be the end of this method of vine-growing. As from 1860, European vines were progressively decimated by a bug named *Phylloxera vastatrix,* and when it was finally discovered that the only solution was to graft European varieties onto naturally resistant American root stock, neat rows were planted, making it possible to work the vineyards with horse-drawn, and later with tractor-powered instruments. For some reason, three tiny plots of ungrafted vines belonging to Bollinger seem to resist the bug, and these are still hand-tilled. Although the fruit of these vines used to be vinified together with Bollinger's other grapes, it was decided, in 1969, to make a special wine from them and to call it Vieilles Vignes Françaises, meaning Old French Vines. This wine is only produced in vintage years, and production is limited.

TASTING

◆ *Special cuvée*
A rich-smelling nose, with more than a hint of dried fruit. The mouth feeling confirms this sensation, with power and structure from an excellent acidity. This very clear-cut, one-of-a-kind style is typical of the house, and the length of the taste feelings are proof of the wine's breeding and quality.

◆ *RD 1982*
Extended aging in contact with yeasts in the bottle shows in the range of aromas reminiscent of a fine bakery, fresh and deep at the same time. Although almost fourteen years old when tasted, this wine seems incredibly young still, from a very fine vintage. A magnificent bottle for the end of the millennium.

its own specific style. Their personality derives from the origin of the grapes and from an unusual combination of very traditional and entirely modern wine-making techniques. Ghislain de Montgolfier, who manages the company, describes this as an introspective process open to modern technology.

Two extremely original wines in Bollinger's range, the RD (which stands for "recently disgorged") and the Vieilles Vignes Françaises, deserve particular attention because both illustrate something fundamental to the house of Bollinger and even to the cause of great wines. By this I mean that kind of

Roederer

The history of the house of Roederer dates back to the eighteenth century, when it was founded by Louis Roederer. One of his descendants, Jean-Claude Rouzaud, manages the company today. This long family history is typical of the majority of Champagne's great houses, even if some of them have recently been acquired by industrial groups with diversified activities.

A visit to Roederer's buildings gives a clear understanding that certain golden ages have marked the aesthetic sense of Champagne companies. These buildings, dating from the early and mid-nineteenth and early twentieth centuries, are especially fine and have been beautifully restored. In the winery and the cellars, a synthesis of beauty and function is attained. The cellar in which Roederer keeps its "reserve wines" is unusual in Champagne, with its impressive lines of huge oak barrels, each one with a different sculpted facade showing a working scene in the vineyards or the cellars. Roederer's choice of keeping reserve wines, destined for blending with younger wines to produce the non-vintage blends, in large wood barrels is unique in Champagne. But this is far from sufficient to explain the high quality of this house's wines. A vineyard sited in some of the best villages of Champagne, extremely careful wine-making and blending, and slow maturing in bottles all contribute their share to the final result. The person who orchestrates this process is the cellar-master, and at Roederer, his name is Michel Pansu. In his opinion, a fine champagne requires three main characteristics:

Opposite: Louis Roederer owns one of the finest vineyards in Champagne, spread across many different villages.
Above: Superb buildings in the center of Reims, perfectly restored.

delicacy, power, and fruit flavors, which should be equally important. This trio forms the basis from which a champagne is blended, as each component comes from a different part of the vineyard. This basis for harmony will enable the individual style of each of Roederer's wines to emerge. For example, the Brut Premier non-vintage will show power, whereas Cristal will tend towards delicacy. The use of wood in the making or the aging of some wines provides a touch to the flavor rather like a signature. Provided the wines are made with the best possible grapes, complexity—the hallmark of a great wine—will develop in time.

When should one drink a great wine? The question makes Michel Pansu smile, as he is not one for ceremony. He remembers one of his greatest tasting experiences, sharing a bottle of Cristal with friends by a mountain stream after a day's trout fishing. The fact that they only had the most basic form of glass to drink from in no way spoiled their pleasure on this occasion. A great wine is almost always linked to a moment of intensity, which does not necessarily mean formal surroundings. Michel Pansu has just one wish for those who taste Cristal: that they derive intense pleasure from the moment. Time will then deal with preserving this moment in terms of memory.

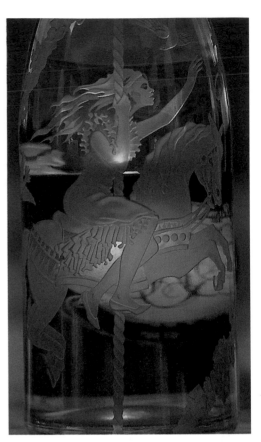

Above: Roederer's offices in Reims.
Right: Engraved magnum of Cristal.
Below: The drawing room.
Opposite: Bottles of Cristal being prepared for disgorgement in the cellars.

TASTING

Roederer is famed above all for its Cristal. This vintage was created in 1876 for the Russian Tsar Alexander II who wanted a special champagne in crystal glass, because of his fear of hidden bombs!

◆ *Cristal 1989*

The nose is clear and precise, tightly strung. The wine is still too young to release its aromatic potential, but it shows hints of dry fruit. In the mouth, one is surprised by the depth of flavor. It seems to have an almost creamy texture which fills the mouth, leaving it fresh at the finish.

◆ *Cristal 1985*

The nose is complex, with layers of fruit and mild spices. In the mouth, the wine seems very young still and is solidly built with plenty of grip that makes the flavors last. There is just a sign that the texture is beginning to soften. Roederer's wines are renowned for their delicacy and elegance.

Krug

The names of a considerable number of Champagne houses are definitely Germanic. A few examples are Krug, Bollinger, Deutz, Taittinger, or Roederer. Such families came to Champagne from the Rhine area between the middle of the eighteenth and the middle of the nineteenth centuries, founding dynasties that have since devoted themselves to producing that famous sparkling white wine that symbolizes France around the world. Today there are four members of the Krug family, from two different generations, working full time in the company that was founded in 1843 by Johann-Joseph Krug. All the house's wines are fermented in small oak barrels in the time-honored way that has become practically extinct in Champagne. Krug's champagnes are made available to markets after aging for much longer in their cellars than those of almost any of their competitors. The taste of Krug is remarkably powerful for a champagne, and the wines are sold at a high price, on a par with their quality and reputation. Rémi Krug speaks of their wines, and of the sensations experienced when tasting a great wine, like few other people. All in all, Krug is a special case in Champagne.

What is the secret of Krug? Is it appropriate to talk about secrets when know-how has been patiently accumulated through quiet determination over the years, enabling a style to emerge which builds and feeds on that experience? Making a great wine implies meticulous care at every stage of the wine-making process and a capacity to react quickly when the unexpected occurs. This takes on a further dimension in the case of a champagne blender, who has to imagine how his wine will taste in two to five years' time.

For Henri Krug, the test is even harder, as the time scale is between eight and ten years, so he is obliged to work with time on his side!

As far as Rémi Krug is concerned, if a combination of soil and climate is what differentiates one wine from another, it is up to the wine-maker to play the variations on a particular theme. His job is to care for each wine and pay attention to details like scraping and cleaning every single barrel. The aim of the exercise is to reveal the potential that lies within the raw material. As an example of this process, one could take the rarest wine of Krug's range, Clos du Mesnil. The general rule in Champagne is that wines from different plots of vines, planted with different grape varieties, are blended together. Here is a champagne made from a single grape, Chardonnay, which comes from a single vineyard surrounded by walls in the village called Le Mesnil. The vineyard was purchased by Krug in 1971 and replanted with a range of different clonal types of the Chardonnay variety. It took fourteen years after this purchase for the first wine from Krug's Clos du Mesnil to be marketed, in 1985. This is proof enough that long-term vision, not to speak of considerable thought and means of all kinds, is necessary for the making of exceptional wines. And may it not be forgotten that a wine, however great it may be, cannot remain so without customers.

The Krugs do not believe that you have to be a wine expert to appreciate great wine. All that is required is a dose of sensitivity and the ability to tune in to one's senses. This sensual capacity will naturally lead into a sort of dialogue with wine. Knowledge may

Opposite: Surrounded by walls, which is the meaning of the French term « clos », the Clos du Mesnil vineyard is ideally situated in the heart of the village of le Mesnil-sur-Oger. This is from a late nineteenth century engraving.
Above: Bottles of Krug patiently waiting for time to do its job.

be added on afterwards, but it is not vital for the amateur. So one can say that Krug is accessible, except for its price. As part of its attention to detail, and to the way customers drink, Krug has spent more time and trouble than any other house on the infinitely detailed subject of harmonizing their wines with food. The considerable presence of Krug champagnes on the wine lists of the world's top restaurants bears witness to this work.

There is something magically unpredictable about the best moment for enjoying the flavors of a fine wine. Rémi Krug likes to quote the experience of an American customer who, after drinking a bottle of Krug's Grande Cuvée with some barbecued spare ribs, found that the wine kept giving off layer after layer of taste sensations, and, said simply " Krug just never ends! "

TASTING

◆ *Krug Grande Cuvée*

This wine is in the range that does not carry a vintage, and which Krug prefers to call "multi-vintage" rather than "non-vintage." Indeed, it is blended from wines of ten different harvests and is considered by the Krugs as the archetype of their wines. They even go so far as to say that if their range had to be reduced to a single wine, this would be the one!

The nose is initially reserved, with a feeling of hidden power. After a few minutes in the glass, a series of complex aromas start to emerge, with alternatively mineral and fruity aspects, lightly smoked. The mouth feel is extraordinary. Initially it runs straight through the palate, gradually building up a series of vibrations between the tongue and the roof of the mouth that are triggered off again each time one takes

another sip of the wine. The overall impression is long and powerful, with so many flavors that it is important to take one's time and let them develop gradually.

◆ *Krug Vintage 1985*

The nose is both more powerful and more expressive than that of the Grande Cuvée. This note certainly corresponds to the 1985 vintage, which sings through like a first violin. The concentration of flavors in the

mouth is considerable and gradually evolves into a long follow-through that finishes fresh and clear. Throughout is the characteristic vibration that is set up by the contrast between power and acidity in all Krug's wines. The texture is very silky and rich, and, as the wine warms up, the layers of aroma peel off, going from fruit to wood and spices. Despite the power of this wine, it stays very refreshing. A truly great champagne.

Opposite (upper): Bottles on the hand-riddling tables. Opposite (lower): The only Champagne house that has a resident barrel-maker. Above (upper): The Clos du Mesnil was acquired by Krug in 1971, and has since been entirely replanted. Above (lower): The barrels are rinsed before harvesttime.

Veuve Clicquot

When a champagne has been known worldwide for more than two centuries and has never abandoned its motto, "Just one quality, the best," it is fascinating to trace its history. Naturally, legends and reality are mixed up in any such story, as are men and events, but history feeds off mythology. Clicquot was founded, as a Champagne company, on January 3, 1772, when Philippe Clicquot published an announcement in the *Gazette de France* saying that he had started a wine merchant's business under his name. Philippe Clicquot was young and ambitious and had plans to develop his business by exporting as soon as possible. This didn't take too long, as the first delivery to Moscow was made in 1780, which was to be the prelude to a phenomenal success story in the Tsar's Russia. In 1798, Philippe's son François entered the business. Twenty-four years old, he had just married Nicole-Barbe Ponsardin. This promising beginning for this wine almost came to a premature halt in 1805, when François Clicquot died. Despite all the odds, as the Napoleonic wars had damaged the young company's major markets in Central and Eastern Europe, his wife decided to keep the company going. Her energy and determination were going to place her name in the history books.

Within four months of the death of her husband, she found business partners and recreated the company under the name Veuve (meaning widow) Clicquot Ponsardin (her maiden name). This was the start of what was to be a long reign but also of a series of major difficulties in the years to come. Being a business woman in the nineteenth century could not have been easy, and

Opposite: In Champagne, the economy of many villages is assured by the purchase of grapes from small growers by the big houses. Above: The cellars in Champagne can be very extensive. They stretch for fifteen miles at Veuve Clicquot.

her family was opposed to her playing such a role. Getting her wines to the markets in Eastern Europe was the main problem, as Napoleonic France was blockaded by the British navy. When peace finally came in 1814, things started to look better, and a ship bearing some of

her cellar-master. It was she who set the house's motto of "Just one quality, the best."

Nowadays, Veuve Clicquot's vineyard covers 707 acres, and as with all the very large houses in Champagne, grapes are also purchased to make wine. Pinot Noir

varieties, are vinified separately so that Jacques Peters, the cellar-master, can work with as wide a palette as possible when deciding upon his blend.

Although the soil in Champagne can be chalky and often lies very thin on the sub-soil, the vines grow vigorously and have

the 1811 vintage, which was to acquire a great reputation, was able to leave the port of Le Havre for St. Petersburg. Other ships followed, as demand grew rapidly for Madame Clicquot's wines, particularly in Russia, where almost a million bottles a year were consumed in the 1870's. Madame Clicquot's fame and wealth became such that she was named "La Grande Dame de la Champagne," or "Champagne's Great Lady." The invention of riddling, which is the tricky process by which the deposit formed in bottles of champagne after the secondary fermentation is brought to the bottle-neck to be eliminated, is attributed to her or to

has the largest share of the vineyard surface and is planted in the "Montagne de Reims" and upper Marne Valley areas. This is the grape that gives power and structure to the Clicquot style, which is softened, in the case of the non-vintage wines, by some Pinot Meunier, a grape which has tender fruit flavors. Chardonnay, from the "Côte des Blancs," add freshness and elegance to the blends. Champagne vineyards, like those of Burgundy, are divided into a multitude of plots, often very small, and the Clicquot vineyards are no exception. The grapes from their 340 plots, planted with one or another of the three authorized grape

to be restrained by severe pruning in winter. Pruning serves several functions: restraining growth so that the grapes produced can ripen properly, guiding the plant so it maintains balance between young and older parts, and extending its life span by eliminating older or damaged

Opposite (above and below): The reception rooms at Clicquot's private house, initially built by Edouard Werlé, who succeeded Madame Clicquot.
Above: Madame Clicquot herself.
Below: These barrels, no longer in use, show the names of vine plots within the villages that have always been used in Clicquot's blends.

parts. Mr. Renard, Clicquot's vineyard manager, says that one has to make the plant suffer just a little in order to produce the best possible fruit.

When making non-vintage champagne, wines are put into reserve from good years to be blended with those from years to come. These "reserve wines" may form over thirty percent of a non-vintage blend. They help ensure that the house style is maintained, year after year, and they may be kept for as long as six or seven years in special tanks before being incorporated in the blend. Clicquot was acquired a few years ago by a large luxury group, and hopefully the personality and the quality of its wines will survive the efficient financial logic of the new owners.

Last but not least, the most visible sign of the brand is the deep yellow label that makes its non-vintage wine stand out on a shelf from yards away. It certainly was a masterpiece of marketing to have used so much strong color in a label that goes back to the nineteenth century, and no one would change it today. If you think that the color should be called orange, you should refer to the original description of the precise tone to be used, in the days before colors were industrially coded with coldly barbaric numbers and letters. The color is described as: "the yellow of an egg which comes from a chicken having been fed on corn grain." Poetry can be so precise.

TASTING

◆ *La Grande Dame 1988*
This wine illustrates perfectly the degree of harmony that the best wines from Champagne can achieve. The nose appears fresh and full, with notes of flowers and ripe fruit, underlined by a lightly toasted touch. The mouth feel is smooth and lively, with considerable complexity and perfect balance as it gradually fades.

La Romanée

Burgundy's vineyards stretch from the town of Auxerre, at the northern extremity, almost to the city of Lyon to the south, over a total distance of more than 185 miles. This may seem quite extensive, but in fact these vineyards are divided up into many subregions, precisely defined and of variable sizes, which are sometimes separated by considerable distances. In fact, the total surface area that may produce Burgundy's wines is much smaller than that of Bordeaux, although it contains twice as many distinct appellations, some of them tiny.

Vines were probably planted here in Roman times, but it is certain that the local production was well-known during the reign of Charlemagne at the turn of the eighth and ninth centuries. Later on, the Burgundian dukes, who ruled what was later a part of France, carried their wines all over Europe, using them extensively to nourish followers and armies, but also to help get treaties signed! This did much for the reputation of Burgundy. The quality of the wines of Burgundy owes a great deal to two monastic orders that developed here from the tenth century onwards: Cluny and Cîteaux. Princes and kings demanded wines from Burgundy for their cellars, and, in modern times, merchant houses organized the trade and started to export burgundy around the world.

In the heart of Burgundy lies its most famous area, La Côte d'Or, which means "the golden slope." This is a narrow band of hillside running from Dijon to the village of Santenay, about thirty five miles, and at its narrowest point merely half a kilometer. It is divided into two parts. The Côte de Nuits runs between Dijon and a point north of Beaune and produces almost exclusively red wines. Around the town of Beaune and to its south lies the Côte de Beaune, which produces both red and white wines. At various

Above: Vines of La Romanée, France's smallest "appellation contrôlée," in their glorious autumnal colors.

points in the Côte d'Or, one finds those single vineyards whose names are sufficient to make a wine connoisseur's mouth water: La Romanée, La Romanée-Conti, Le Chambertin, Le Montrachet, and so on. Such vineyards became so famous in the nineteenth century that the nearest villages asked to change their original names in order to benefit from the aura of these magic words that were so much better known than the villages themselves. Thus Gevrey became Gevrey-Chambertin, and Vosne became Vosne-Romanée, for instance. These top vineyards constitute a category known as Grands Crus. Although they only account for two percent of burgundy and are sold for very high prices, they show the logic of the ranking system bequeathed on each vine plot, which is classified according to a quality potential that has been analyzed over a long time span.

La Romanée, with pigeon accompanied by chestnuts and figs, at Bernard Morillon's restaurant in Beaune.

Each Grand Cru is in fact an appellation in its own right, and the village on whose land it is sited does not appear in the appellation. The smallest of all of France's appellations is one of these Grands Crus, formed by just one hectare of land, called La Romanée. It belongs to the Ligier-Belair family and lies within the commune (or parish) of Vosne-Romanée. Around it are a number of vineyard plots also classified as Grands Crus and, a little further from the epicenter, a series of vineyards that have the status of Premiers Crus. This is the second level in the hierarchy, and such wines will show the village name before that of the Premier Cru vineyard. The third level is that of village wines, which will just have the name of the village: Vosne-Romanée in this example. At the fourth level are wines which will bear the name of the subregion, in this case Côte de Nuits, and finally, generally from outlying

vineyards, the wines are simply called bourgogne, or burgundy. The higher the ranking of the wine, the smaller the vineyard area that qualifies for that rank and the more restrictive the constraints imposed on the wine's production.

La Romanée is directly above the vineyard of La Romanée-Conti, on the slopes of the hill known as Vosne. At this point, the slope is at its steepest, and the soil is correspondingly thin and dry. Is this the explanation for the fact that La Romanée's wines seem more delicate than those of its neighbor? In any event, tasting La Romanée is sufficient proof that wines which appear delicate can reveal considerable underlying power when they come from "terroirs" of this quality.

TASTING

◆ *La Romanée 1993*
The nose is full of aromas of dark berry fruit and spices, with a hint of smoke and earth. This complex mixture is dense and airy at the same time. The taste is clear and fresh, with an extremely precise definition of the flavors. It seems at first to be more delicate than powerful, but the wine has considerable length and its texture is extremely fine. A very clean finish confirms the first impression of relative delicacy and pureness.

◆ *La Romanée 1992*
This wine has rather less complexity on the nose, with hints of softer fruit and spices. This lighter feeling is confirmed in the mouth by a wine that needs, like all potentially great wines, to be left in the glass for a while to develop its full aromatic potential. It appears still very young and has excellent fruit flavors, which finish on a firm note that comes from its tannins.

◆ *La Romanée 1989*
A few additional years in the bottle have enabled this wine to evolve and show some of that velvety opulence that is so

characteristic of fine burgundy. The nose shows a mixture of power and finesse. The components evaporate in successive layers to reveal ripe fruit, smoke, and a mixture of woodland and mushroom smells. This complexity is very much present in the mouth, with a silky feel to it, and great lift. An image of a bowl of fruit refreshed by morning appears in the mind's eye, and the sensations last for many seconds, giving intense pleasure.

ROMANÉE
CONTI

La Romanée-Conti

In the heart of the Côte de Nuits, the Domaine de La Romanée-Conti is sole owner of two of Vosne-Romanée's Grands Crus: La Romanée-Conti and La Tâche. In addition to this, the estate is the largest owner of vineyards in four other Grands Crus from the same village: Richebourg, Romanée St. Vivant, Grands Echezeaux, and Echezeaux. As if such a concentration of the finest red vineyards in Burgundy seemed a little out of balance, they also own a small plot of the most famous white vineyard in the Côte de Beaune, Montrachet.

Approaching such a prestigious estate, whose wines are among the most expensive and sought-after in the world, is far from an everyday experience and involves a quiver of expectancy. What surprises one at first is the extreme simplicity of the buildings, hidden away behind a simple gate in a small village street. This austerity is perfectly in tune with the modesty that prevails on the estate, which considers itself, in some respects, a successor of those monks who worked these vineyards for centuries, neither for wealth nor for glory. Aubert de Villaine, the joint manager, is quite happy with the term of great wines being applied to the estate's production, insofar as this means that such wines are, by definition, extraordinary and pay a tribute to nature's gift. The fact that Burgundy's vineyards are divided up into a multitude of tiny plots and appellations, combined with the use of a single grape variety, the Pinot Noir, means that man must necessarily take second place to nature. Furthermore, the Pinot Noir grape will tend to reveal differences due to "terroir," rather than mask them.

Opposite: The village of Vosne, seen from the vineyard of La Romanée-Conti.
Above: The gateway of Domaine de La Romanée-Conti, or DRC for the initiated.

The story of the Grands Crus of Burgundy is one of vineyards that have proved, over the centuries, their capacity to produce exceptional wines, aided by accumulated experience and the will to make the best wine possible. Without this objective, nothing would have been possible. The monks had time on their hands, curiosity for the workings of nature, and the ability to learn, but above all they were not tied by an obligation to make financial profit from their vineyards. Perhaps man's role today should take some inspiration from these modest observers of nature who respected its phenomena without trying to impose their will. Nevertheless, managing an estate of this kind requires a clear idea of goals in terms of wine-making, as well as an awareness of one's limits.

Aubert de Villaine believes that eighty percent of a wine stems from its natural ingredients, transformed or alchemized by the "terroir." Therefore, his principal preoccupation lies with the vineyard and the natural balance necessary to its environment. At the Domaine de La Romanée-Conti, soil is regenerated with natural compost, made the previous year from shredded vine trimmings, residues from the wine press, and a little manure as an activator. This ensures that the soil's bacterial life is as healthy as possible. There are about fifty different varieties of the Pinot Noir plant in the vineyards. Such natural diversity, while rare, is important as a basis for observation, for improved natural resistance to disease, and for added complexity in flavors.

The vine plant must be severely pruned to produce good wine, otherwise there will be too much leaf growth, and grapes will not ripen fully. Spraying against the various diseases and pests that beset all plants is kept to a minimum and restricted to biological products. The same attitude prevails during the wine-making process, with a policy of minimal intervention by man or machine, so that the grape naturally reveals its own flavors.

What are the greatest wine experiences of Aubert de Villaine? His reply is that the difference between a great wine and a good wine lies in its degree of intensity. There are wines that will have an immediate impact simply through the strength of their personality. He remembers experiencing this with different wines, such as a 1921 Yquem, a 1953 Pétrus, or several great Hermitages. The first wine from his own estate that springs to his memory is a 1962 La Tache, when tasted three years after its harvest. For those of us who rarely experience wines of this order, such memories may appear closer to myth than reality, but the key point is the relationship between one wine and another within an individual's experience. There can be no absolutes in this field, as everybody has their own taste and preferences.

Left: The wines spend around eighteen months in new oak barrels.
Below: A small bunch of grapes called "verjus," deliberately left behind by the pickers as unripe.
Below left: After barrel aging, wines age for at least an additional year in bottles before being shipped.

HORIZONTAL TASTING
OF DIFFERENT WINES
OF THE DOMAINE DE LA ROMANÉE-
CONTI FROM A SINGLE VINTAGE.
ALL THESE WINES WERE IN BARRELS
AT THE TIME OF TASTING.

◆ *Grands-Échezeaux 1994*
The nose is full of intense fruit aromas
with hints of spices coming through.
The mouth is in perfect harmony
with this impression and adds that lovely
suave texture specifically found
in great burgundies.

◆ *Romanée-Saint-Vivant 1994*
The aromas are concentrated but very fine.
They seemed more restrained for the
moment, with a lacelike delicacy.
In the mouth, the flavors are remarkably
precise, and the overall feel is powerful,
with plenty of grip from some strong
tannins. The fruit flavors surround this
and are long-lasting.

◆ *Richebourg 1994*
One is immediately surprised by the
powerfully spicy character of the aromas,

which are strongly evocative of dark colors.
A lighter note is added by concentrated red
and black berry fruit. The mouth sensation
is structured and almost angular.
It appears relatively austere, compared to
the first two wines, and will probably
last longer.

◆ *La Tâche 1994*
Although apparently darker in color than
the Richebourg, its nose is more delicate
but harder to describe, with flower, fruit,
and mineral aromas. The mouth feel is
smooth and silky, with an almost creamy
texture. This rich sensation is reinforced by
intense fruit flavors and the firm
concentration typical of young red wines of
this category.

◆ *La Romanée-Conti 1994*
Its nose is more reserved than that of its
cousins from different vineyards. Austerity
is the key word, but one can perceive
underlying black fruit aromas of
considerable power. What strikes one in
tasting this wine is the wonderful balance
between its elements. Very powerful, while
remaining elegant and fresh, it manages to
seem concentrated without being
aggressive. This is undoubtedly a very
great wine which, in time, will reveal its
full potential.

Wines of this level are necessarily rare,
partly because of the extremely limited size
of the vineyards. They are an example of
what can be produced in Burgundy.

Le Montrachet de Bouchard Père et Fils

The most famous dry white wine in the world comes from a very small vineyard that covers precisely 21,713 acres in Burgundy's Côte de Beaune, divided between the twin villages of Puligny-Montrachet and Chassagne-Montrachet. As is generally the case in Burgundy, this vineyard is also subdivided between several owners of very small plots of varying sizes, sometimes just a few rows of vines. Bouchard Père et Fils owns one of the largest of these plots, situated right in the center of Le Montrachet and covering about two point five acres. It was purchased by the Bouchards in 1838, and if it were to be sold today, its market value would probably be in the vicinity of 150 million dollars!

What makes this wine so great? The name Montrachet means bald mountain, which is a qualification for the extremely thin top soil on this outcrop of calcareous rock that makes it just about incapable of producing any other crop than wine grapes. One variety in particular was hardy enough to flourish on such inhospitable territory: chardonnay. This grape is particularly adaptable and proves once again that the finest wines often come from vineyards which are at or near the limits imposed by climate for ripening grapes. The exceptional quality of wines from the Montrachet vineyard comes from their considerable concentration that, in turn, enables them to last for many years. Montrachet was the only dry white wine selected in 1787 by Thomas Jefferson, the future president of the United States, to be part of his list of France's greatest wines.

The house of Bouchard Père et Fils currently owns 321 acres of vineyards in Burgundy, of which 213 are of Premier or Grand Cru status. In the depths of their cellars, which are those of the former Château de Beaune, lies what must be the most fabulous collection of old vintages of burgundies, both red and white. Some of these go back to the nineteenth century and are still full of flavors. Such wines are a living memory of Burgundy's history, and possessing such a collection gives the owner a rare historical perspective. For Joseph Henriot, the current owner, great wine is very much a part of culture, as much as music or painting. The same process of learning to appreciate and then comparing one's feelings when confronted by the work of different artists applies to fine wines. Preferring a Renoir to a Gauguin may of course depend on the painting, but it also has much to do with the individual taste of the spectator, the mood he is in, and his knowledge of painting. After all, a number of music lovers consider that Beethoven's string quartets have more depth and pureness than any of his better known symphonies. All this is a matter of style, taste, and experience, whether music, painting or wine be concerned.

A great wine can only be defined in comparison with a good wine. What does the one have that the other lacks? Clearly the

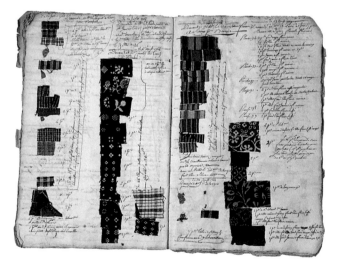

Opposite: Part of the Montrachet vineyard, with Chevalier Montrachet, another Grand Cru, in the background.
Above: The Bouchard family were cloth merchants before buying vineyards and starting to trade in wines, in 1731, in the town of Beaune. Their sales catalog of that time reminds one of the patchwork of the Côte d'Or vineyards.

Above: The barrel cellar for white wines at Bouchard Père et Fils. Somewhere along this row there are a few barrels of Montrachet.
Below: An early price list of the house founded by Michel Bouchard and his son, Joseph.

superiority of the best wines comes from their greater concentration, finesse, and aging capacity. These elements are all tangible, because they can be perceived by the taster. Thus it is sufficient to say that a great wine can be identified, first and foremost, by its taste relative to others. But there is another element, far harder to measure with any degree of precision, which is the mythical aspect of a wine. This is a by-product of its history, often linked to scarcity and high price, and is very much a part of the majority of great wines. Particular circumstances will often bring out a series of material and immaterial aspects of a wine in the memory of the taster, thereby creating a form of sublimation. Joseph Henriot is fully convinced that a wine's history is an essential part of its reputation. Good wines give many a joy and pleasure to the wine-lover, whereas great wines not only contribute greater intensity to these

moments, but also add a cultural dimension.

Burgundy's great wines, such as Montrachet, have their individual characteristics, but they also evoke the memory of those monks who, for centuries, cultivated the same pieces of land to provide a rare moment for those who have the good fortune to taste the wine. Particular benchmarks for excellence can change and will definitely vary from one culture to another, but it remains true that the ability for any wine to exist for tens, or even hundreds of years, constantly giving the impression to those who drink it that they are experiencing something exceptional, is a sign of a great wine. Without any doubt, Montrachet is one such wine.

Tasting

◆ *Montrachet 1993*

The nose of this wine has a sharp edge which makes one think of a bowl of fruit with a mineral tang to it. It is as if the soil and bedrock showed through the layer of fruit. After a few moments in the glass, the wine liberates a series of richer and more complex aromas, reminiscent of butter. The mouth feel is vertical and somewhat austere. This is perfectly understandable in a wine tasted well before its phase of maturity, which will start between the years 2000 and 2010.

The liveliness of the wine apparent from its smell is confirmed in the mouth, with very clear-cut aromas that last for a considerable time.

◆ *Montrachet 1990*

An extra three years in the bottle and a harvest of superior quality compared to the previous wine have given this wine a chance to show a bit more of its potential. The nose seems ampler and richer. The mineral edge has filled out with an exuberant bouquet of ripe fruit, followed by whiffs of toasted bread and hazelnuts. The taste is luscious and totally fills the mouth, with good structure. This rich feeling lasts a long time, with some warmth and a finish that is pleasantly fresh and balanced.

◆ *Montrachet 1989*

This was also a sunny year. One can almost feel the heat of the sun through the exotically fruity aromas that fill the nose. The mouth feel is even more developed and full than the 1990, without the slightest trace of austerity. This is a wine destined for instant pleasure, very rich and supple in its fruit. Voluptuous and luxurious.

Tasting
Burgundy's great wines

In Burgundy the wine-maker does not impose his will on the vineyards. He must reveal the individual character of each of his wines by making the most of the particular combination of climate, soil, and grapes that nature has given him. Raw material is of top quality, but scarce, and there is only one variety of grape. All this means that it is impossible to balance a wine by blending in wines from different vineyard lots or grape varieties, as is the case in Bordeaux, for example. Both grapes and vineyard plots are entirely at the mercy of Mother Nature in Burgundy, because the conditions are so specific. This makes it easier to understand why a particular Burgundian wine can vary considerably in its taste from one year to the next.

Domaine Weinbach

Domaine Weinbach is one of the all too rare wine estates to be run by women. This would not be a sufficient reason on its own to qualify the wines it produces as among the world's best, but it so happens that we are faced here with a range of wines of incomparable charm and finesse, a magnificent estate and vineyard, and the exceptional personality of the Faller family. As is often the case with a great wine estate, it is the accumulation of a series of components, often apparently insignificant, that produces a whole which becomes much more than the sum of its parts.

The name Weinbach comes from a small stream that flows through the property. Its significance is manifest, as it means "the river of wine." The home and winery of the Fallers is called "Le Clos des Capucins" and was built in 1612 by Capuchin monks. Above it rises the Schlossberg hill, where vines have been cultivated for maybe a thousand years. In any case, the earliest written traces of Schlossberg as a vineyard go back to the fifteenth century, and it was the first of Alsace's Grands Crus to be officially instated, in 1975. On just under fifty acres, Domaine Weinbach produces most of the wide range that can be made in Alsace, where wines, unusually for France, bear the name of their grape variety on the label. Riesling, Gewurztraminer, Pinot Gris, and Muscat, sometimes from late harvests, or "vendanges tardives," are the leaders of the pack with the Faller ladies, but they also make delicious Pinot Blanc and Sylvaner, those

Opposite: The Clos des Capucins, with the "Weinbach," or "river of wine," in the foreground. The slope of the Schlossberg hill is just visible to the right.
Above: The estate's cellar, with its large barrels, or tuns, traditionally used in Alsace.

wonderful thirst-quenchers that are one of Alsace's specialties. The mark of the Weinbach Rieslings is elegance, and their Gewurztraminers are among the most sumptuous available.

Visits to wine estates are too often filled with a display of technical details such as the latest piece of equipment for torturing grapes. In such cases, as often as not, the visit concludes with a tasting in either a damp cellar or a clinically cold tasting room. In either event, one struggles from the cold and from not being able to sit down. This may be excellent for testing physical resistance but is not exactly a lot of fun. Things do not happen this way at Domaine Weinbach, where you are invited into the house and shown into a cozy living room, where the wood paneling and furniture exude the traditional warmth of an Alsatian household. In the next room, or around the same table, there will probably be another group of pilgrims who have come from as far and wide as Japan, the United States, Germany, or Italy, united by their love of good wine. From the kitchen behind come the sounds and smells of the forthcoming lunch. The wines arrive, one by one, and are poured by Colette Faller or one of her daughters, Catherine or Laurence. They are tasted, compared, and discussed, and the necessary time is given to this moment of concentration. Meanwhile, back in the kitchen, the preparations for lunch require Madame Faller's attentions just as much as the tastings. Wine is a part of everyday life here, no more and no less. Delicacy and attentiveness to others characterize Colette Faller, and it could be said that this also applies to her wines. They do not bang the drum so much as tiptoe onto one's palate. Nuance is the name of the game, although the depth of a wine such as the Riesling Schlossberg leaves no doubt about its capacity to age considerably.

When Colette Faller talks about tasting a wine, she suggests that one should close one's eyes in order to concentrate on the sensations received, as with a kiss. When talking about wine-making, she says that a grower should love his vines and be with them, year in, year out, as with her children. She believes that a great wine will show its quality in its youth, and that time will simply add the patina of years, without transforming its veritable nature. Her younger daughter, Laurence, who makes the wines, adds that a great wine should, above all, give pleasure to those who drink it. If the quality of a wine is often considered to be linked with a high degree of richness and concentration, one should not forget that complexity and harmony are also involved. The Fallers do not make wines according to hard and fast rules, as if following a recipe. They prefer to pay attention to the nature of the particular variety of grape, which will interpret, in its own language, the messages that a particular soil and climate transmit. Low yields and a respect for nature are part of the rules at Weinbach. Each parcel, and in some cases, each vat, will be treated separately in the case of the top wines, so you may find, in a given vintage, two or three different Riesling Sainte Catherine or Riesling Schlossberg, each bearing a number. This gives you the rare possibility to choose the wine preferred, provided that you are quick enough, as the supply is never sufficient to meet demand.

TASTING

◆ *Riesling cuvée Sainte Catherine (1) 1994*
*The nose is so delicate that indeed it helps
to close one's eyes to identify its nuances.
The silkiness of its texture is remarkable.
Gentle aromas of young fruit linger on the
palate, helped by the wine's freshness.*

◆ *Riesling cuvée Sainte Catherine (2) 1994*
*The nose has a mineral edge that
distinguishes it from the previous wine
and gives it additional power. The mouth
feel is richer and more rounded, with a very
long finish that vibrates with flavor and is
perfectly balanced. A top class wine.*

◆ *Gewurztraminer cuvée Laurence 1994*
*A sumptuously aromatic nose, typical
of this grape variety, with a strong hint of
roses and a spicy edge. It has as much
concentration as most late harvest versions.
The taste is also full of aromas and fills
the mouth completely without seeming
over-weighty at any point. Its extremely
fine texture fills the mouth.*

◆ *Riesling sélection de grains nobles 1990*
*This is probably the rarest of wines
in Alsace, as Riesling requires much more
sunshine than Gewurztraminer or Pinot*

*Gris to attain the sugar levels necessary
for a late harvest wine. Only small amount
is made in exceptional years. The nose
is very tightly-knit and yet extremely
aromatic. One can pick out notes of exotic
fruit and honey, with a hint of smoke.
The mouth manages to reconcile richness
and freshness. All the finesse of the
Riesling grape has been concentrated here,
and the complexity of the wine comes
through gradually, perfectly balanced
and absolutely delicioius.*

**Above (upper): The bell tower
of the church in the neighboring village of
Kaysersberg.**
**Above: The main building of the Clos des
Capucins, which includes house, cellars,
and winery.**
**Opposite: Lunch is being prepared in the
Faller kitchen. Will it be choucroute or
baeckeoffe?**
**Right: A typically Alsatian house in
Kaysersberg.**

Zind-Humbrecht

Vines draw their full substance from the soil on which they grow, and the mineral and organic material that it contains, according to the natural rhythm of the seasons. Grape harvest is the logical culmination of the growth cycle and requires all the energy available on the estate. It is now too late to speculate on what the weather might do, as picking has begun and must be minutely followed, plot by plot, and the grapes sorted, transported, and crushed prior to wine-making. This is not the best time to visit a wine-maker, as harvest comes but once a year, but there are plenty of other opportunities during the year that will give you a chance to witness some of the other phases in the vine's cycle. Pruning, bud-burst, flowering, and ripening are all key points in the cycle, and at all times of the year you will probably find Olivier Humbrecht in his vineyards. This is where he most appreciates explaining his job as a wine-maker, as he is convinced that it is above all in the vineyard that a great wine is made.

Léonard Humbrecht put together the family estate by writing vineyards belonging to the Zind and Humbrecht families in 1959. The Humbrechts have been making wine here since the early seventeenth century, and two generations currently work on the estate. Following in the pioneering footsteps of his father, who was convinced, long before others, of the potential of specific "terroirs" in Alsace, Olivier Humbrecht first learned his trade by having a good look at many of the wine-growing areas around the world. This brought him to obtain the prestigious and arduous British diploma of "Master of Wine." In his opinion, the idea of great wine implies a concept that establishes a link between time and nature based on the human element. In other words, the person who tastes the wine plays as great a part as the person who makes the wine. He places an emphasis on two aspects that enable a wine to be considered great : first, its

Above: Antiseptic cellar-plug which enables a visual check on aspects of fermentation in barrels.

**Above:
Le Clos St. Urbain has a slope of sixty eight percent, the steepest in Alsace. While harvesting the grapes, a winch is required to get baskets of grapes up to the track above the vineyard.
Opposite: The Winsbuhl vineyard, near the village of Hunawihr.**

capacity to stand the test of time, in terms of taste, which implies that the wine-maker has considerable accumulated knowledge of its potential and second, the undeniable fact that a wine's reputation usually precedes its taste. The imagination of amateurs will be stimulated and their judgment affected by this. This will be the case however wary they may be of the snobbery that becomes, all too frequently, attached to famous wine labels.

What makes Alsace so unusual in France is the coexistence of different grape varieties on individual vineyard plots, all made into separate wines. A long process of assessing the advantages of particular soil and grape combinations is still going on.

The southernmost vineyard of Alsace, the Rangen of Thann, was first described in the *Grande Chronique de Thann*, written by Malachias Tschamser in the thirteenth

century. He describes the 1232 vintage, for example, as "extremely good: it was so hot that one could have fried an egg on the sandy ground." This south-facing slope is in fact so steep that it forms a right angle with the sun early on in the day and thus is able to generate higher than usual ground temperatures for this latitude. Prior to the destruction of Europe's vineyards by phylloxera, in the

latter part of the nineteenth century, vines covered 1,236 acres of this commune, compared to a mere 35 acres today. This very ancient plot has an extremely poor topsoil, formed of decomposed volcanic and sandy rock, which has the advantage of being highly permeable, thus enabling roots and water to get well underground. Right in the middle of the Rangen vineyard is the Clos St. Urbain, which Léonard Humbrecht purchased in 1970. It produces some extraordinary wines, from either Pinot Gris or Gewurztraminer grape varieties.

The Zind-Humbrecht estate covers, in all, about one hundred acres, which is considerable in Alsatian terms. The appellation Grand Cru d'Alsace designates specific plots of vines, planted only with the best grape varieties. As in Burgundy, such a system is more a presumption of potential quality than an out-and-out guarantee of such quality, but it does identify the precise origin of the wines that carry the vineyard's name. The Humbrecht family has worked hard to find an ideal balance between grape variety and soil in their Grands Crus, planting Gewurztraminer on the rocky and clay soils of Hengst, for example, while keeping Riesling for the more mineral, granite-based Brand vineyard.

TASTING

◆ *Riesling Rangen 1994*
The nose reminds one of flowers in its complexity, but is not yet overtly expressive. The mouth is luxurious from the start, with a long, mineral follow-through, which reminds one of a late-harvest wine.

◆ *Pinot Gris Rangen 1994*
The nose plays the go-between from richness to finesse, sweetness to fruitiness, with touches of mushrooms and minerals. The mouth is perfectly balanced between depth and a refreshingly tangy, mineral-like edge. Its flavors are very long-lasting.

Château d'Arlay

Some landscapes bless the traveler with a sudden and irrepressible feeling of joy, above and beyond well-worn clichés of conventional beauty. This is exactly the feeling given by the countryside around the town of Lons-le-Saunier, roughly mid-way between the town of Beaune and the Swiss border. One can easily imagine why so many battles, both in war and in diplomacy, have been fought for the control of this naturally prosperous region. Rocky outcrops that top densely wooded hills, and peaceful valleys with green pastures carved by fast-flowing streams concur to form a picture of rural France that has probably changed little over past centuries. Before the phylloxera pest swept across Europe, the Jura vineyards covered about 49,420 acres hectares. Nowadays there are only 3,707 of them, spread out to the north and the south of the town of Lons. Local wine-making traditions, as in so many parts of Europe, can be traced back to Roman times, when the emperor Probus, surely one of wine's great benefactors, decided to camp in the area before launching an attack on the central tribes of Gaul. As thanks for their loyalty, the local tribe, known as the Séquanes, were allowed, in 278 A.D., to replant vineyards which one of Probus' predecessors, Domitian, had ordered to be uprooted in the year 92. So one can trace the Jura vineyard back at least to that date, with a further testimony coming from a local church dating from the sixth century and dedicated to St. Vincent, the vine-grower's patron saint.

Opposite: Light and shade, power and subtlety are found in the landscapes of Arlay as they are in its most famous wine.
Above: Count Renaud de Laguiche, who has dedicated his life to his estate and its wines, in his library.

Château d'Arlay was founded as a seigniory in the ninth century and in all probability is the oldest wine-producing château in France and possibly in the world as it has never ceased its vine-growing activities. Even more unusually, it has never been sold, as its successive owners have always handed it on from one family to another. A decisive moment in its wine-making history was when one of the Counts of Chalon-Arlay returned from a Crusade with a yellow-white grape variety called Savagnin, which was to give birth to that most distinctive Jura wine, the extremely long-lived Vin Jaune. This wine cannot be made every year, but when conditions are right, after about seven years spent in barrels, the bottle life of Vin Jaune can exceed one hundred years. Proof of this exceptional longevity abounds. At the 1868 Universal Exposition of Paris, a bottle of Vin Jaune won a gold medal. It came from the 1774

vintage, and so was a mere ninety four years old at the time. More recently, a group of experts tasted a bottle of the very same wine, by then aged 200 years, and they noted that its flavors persisted for almost thirty seconds in the mouth, and

considered that it had at least another century ahead of it!

In many ways, Vin Jaune is an exception to the general rules that govern modern wine-making. Together with another wine produced in tiny quantities in the Jura, Vin

de Paille, it constitutes a reminder of wine-making techniques of past centuries that have simply died out in most other regions. Most wines are now protected, to a large extent, from contact with air. Vin Jaune spends years in barrels which are

not even topped-up to replace the fraction that naturally evaporates. The grapes are picked as late as possible, often after the first snowfalls, in order to let the sugar levels build up as high as possible. This late harvesting procedure in a cold climate gave the wine the local name of "frosted wine" and results in a higher than usual alcoholic content, which enables it to last for much longer than an ordinary wine. Once fermentation is over, the wine is transferred to old tuns, with an air space of at least 1.3 gallons left at the top. The barrels are then sealed, and, with a bit of luck, a bacterial veil will form on the

wine's surface that gives it a special nutty flavor while preventing it from turning to vinegar. A legal minimum of six and a half years in its barrels are necessary before Vin Jaune can be bottled, and there is no guarantee that a barrel will reach the end of this period safe and sound. Vin Jaune's bottle is as unusual as its making. Called a "clavelin," it has a capacity of twenty one ounces, compared with the standard size of twenty five ounces for other wines. This is another relic from former times, as it corresponds to the old imperial pint measurement.

At Château d'Arlay, the Vin Jaune is made in a special cellar, isolated from the other wines produced on the estate. Unlike other wines, temperature fluctuations are not harmful and may indeed be beneficial to its curious way of maturing. In any event, the particular breed of bacteria required to make it would be extremely harmful to any other wine. All in all, Vin Jaune is one of the world's most unusual and rare wines. The classic wine and food associations for Vin Jaune use local recipes, such as poultry with morels or Comté cheese, but its strong and exotic flavors make it a possible running companion for such notorious wine-killers as caviar, sea-urchins, curry, and even chocolate!

Tasting

◆ *Vin Jaune 1985*
The color is dark yellow, almost amber, but extremely bright. The nose is almost impossible to describe, with hints of dried fruit (walnuts are often used to describe these wines), flowers, soft spices and beeswax. The mouth is an amazing combination of power and airy lightness, despite the fact it is 13.5 percent alcohol. The flavors are just as complex as on the nose, with a specifically currylike taste that rounds off the palate. Chemistry specialists say that this is not merely a figment of the taster's imagination.

Opposite (upper): The existing château dominates the village of Arlay.
Opposite (lower): The vineyards slope away from the outer walls of the ruined medieval château.
Above (upper): Alain de Laguiche, who manages the estate, also has a fabulous collection of falcons.
Above (lower): Vin Jaune slowly matures in the vaulted cellars of Château d'Arlay.

Château-Grillet

Château-Grillet's vineyard extends to around 7.5 acres and is thus one of France's smallest appellation contrôlée. Contrary to some legends, however it is not the smallest. This honor goes to La Romanée, which covers less than one hectare, or slightly over 2 acres.

As to the history of the vineyard, it is more than probable that the Romans, who were very thorough explorers of every part of Gaul, planted vineyards here and shipped wines down the Rhône to the Mediterranean, and thus to Rome. Archeological proofs have been found in the neighboring vineyard of Côte Rotie. Much later, during the seventeenth century, the property of Château-Grillet belonged to an engineer called Desargues, who shared with his friend Blaise Pascal such a passion for mathematics that wine-making had to take the back seat. It was not until the eighteenth century that its reputation became established, on a regular basis, as one of France's greatest white wines. In the early part of the twentieth century, Curnonsky, who was known as "The Prince of Gastronomes," considered that Château-Grillet deserved third place amongst France's greatest white wines, after such names as Château d'Yquem and Montrachet, and just before Coulée de Serrant.

The abruptly steep slopes that form Côte Rôtie continue southwards to the small town of Condrieu, around which there is a beautiful vineyard bearing the same name, planted exclusively with a white grape variety called Viognier. Within the Condrieu vineyard area, Château-Grillet has its own identity, and in fact

Opposite: Overlooking the Rhône River, the vineyards of Château-Grillet are laid out like a terraced garden.
Above: The dining room stays cool even in summer.

preceded Condrieu by four years as an official appellation contrôlée. Its name comes from a modest looking manor-house, part of which was fortified under the reign of France's Louis XIII, in the early part of the seventeenth century.

Its vineyard is divided up into a series of tiny terraced plots that climb up the steep slope from the road near the river Rhône. These vines are exceptionally well-situated, forming a sort of amphitheater surrounding the house and facing south. Since 1820, Château-Grillet has belonged to the same family, which has looked after it carefully, rather like a private garden. At the outset of the 1994 harvest, Isabelle Baratin took over from her father and gradually became involved in every aspect of the estate. From spring to autumn, the house becomes a family home, ringing to the sound of children's bicycles and full of the smells of lilac and other things that memories are made of. The vineyard and wine-making activities

have always been part of family life in the country for Isabelle Baratin, just like gardening and making jams. So much so that she appears almost embarrassed when it is suggested that her wine is exceptional. In fact, the vineyards are almost like an extension of the garden, and its terraced walls have to be maintained just like any garden walls.

What is so unusual in this vineyard, besides its slope and the way it is laid out, is the soil. Formed of a particular type of granite-based sand, which is shiny and almost slippery under foot, this soil is extremely permeable to rain water, which means that the violent rainstorms that fall during the summer do not wash away the topsoil, but soak down quickly to the vine roots. As soon as the sun comes out, one can feel the temperature rise like in a greenhouse, as the vines at Grillet are sheltered from the cool northerly winds, and the walls and soil retain the sun's day heat, releasing it during the night. The

Above: The château's tiny cellar.
Below: The Romans shipped their amphoras of wine down the Rhône to Marseille.
Opposite: Some of the stone stairs that lead from one terrace to another date back to Roman times.

◆ *Château-Grillet 1993*
The nose shows a wide range of aromas: flowers, fresh and dried fruit, and a flinty touch. The feeling in the mouth is very smooth, with a firm basis which reminds one of Grillet's soil. Still very young, the wine is a mysterious mixture of austerity and opulence. How long will it take for the mystery to be resolved?

coolest place at this time of year is the château's underground cellar.

The production from such a tiny vineyard is obviously very limited, with a maximum of 12,000 bottles produced in the most generous years. Wine-making is a necessarily slow process here, and the wine spends eighteen months in barrels that are not made of new oak, to avoid marking the wine overmuch. Curiously, although Château-Grillet produces a wine that keeps very well, there is practically

no stock of older vintages at the estate. Continuous demand and lack of space are probably the main causes. The admirable continuity of Château-Grillet is perfectly expressed by its label, which keeps to the perfectly simple and sober design, barely modified, that it originally had in 1830.

É. Guigal

The name of Côte-Rôtie means literally "the roasted hillside." This is a very good description of what happens when the summer sun meets the eastern extremities of Mount Pilat as it dives towards the Rhône River. As one first sees these hillsides, coming south from the city of Lyons, there is already a feel of the Mediterranean, several hundred miles further south.

The first people to plant vines here saw clearly that the site was ideal. Nobody seems quite sure whether these people were Romans, Greeks who came to Marseilles before the Romans, or a local tribe called the Allobroges. What is certain is that the Côte-Rôtie vineyards were already well-known by the first century A.D., as its wines were shipped to Rome, traveling down to the Mediterranean along the Rhône. Pliny the Younger considered these wines so good that they represented serious competition for those from the Latium area around Rome. Geographically, however, the two vineyards are very different. The softly rounded hills that surround Rome are a far cry from the steep, rocky slopes of Côte-Rôtie, whose angle reaches fifty five degree, reminding one of the spectacular vineyards of parts of Alsace, the Mosel Valley in Germany, or the upper Douro in Portugal. The narrow roads twist and turn around the contours of the hillside, and you may well see an ancient micocoulier, or nettle tree, far from its usual Mediterranean home, but proof enough of the exceptionally warm climate here, a mere twelve miles south of Lyons.

Down below the vineyards, on the edge of the Rhône, is the Château d'Ampuis. This Château used to belong to the Haranque family, whose motto was "Nul bien sans peine," meaning "Nothing good without effort." What could be more appropriate to describe the process of producing wine in Côte-Rôtie? This is particularly true of the most authentic part of the appellation, which is planted on 395 acres of terraced slopes facing the river. Its recent success has caused an overextension of the vineyard onto the plateau behind, which cannot produce wine of the same quality. The hillside vineyards are alternatively made up of limestone, granite, or slate-based soils. They are extremely hard to work, and most operations can only be carried out by hand. Traditionalists in viticulture, like Marcel Guigal, weed their plots by hand, refusing to use chemical weed-killers. Just imagine what it must be like carrying hods of fresh grapes to the nearest road on such a slope during harvest! Well, there haven't always been so many roads through the vineyards, and when Étienne Guigal, Marcel's father, who later founded the house, started working as a vineyard hand at age sixteen, he carried every hod all the way down the hill to the winery. This vineyard plot, which belonged at the time to Vidal-Fleury who employed Étienne Guigal, is called La Turque and now belongs to Guigal. Specializing in Rhône Valley wines, this house has succeeded in attaining a worldwide reputation through its Côte-Rôtie and Condrieu wines. Its short history reads like a saga, but its reality has been based on hard work, doing a good job in every department and close observing

Opposite: The vineyard of La Landonne with its traditional individual pole supports for each vine, called "echalas."
Above: The Château d'Ampuis, recently acquired by Marcel Guigal.

nature. Starting production of Côte-Rôtie wines fifty years ago was no surefire bet. Phylloxera and two world wars had taken their toll and the vineyard was in bad shape. The wines sold for one franc (twenty cents) a liter at that time, which was obviously absurd in relation to the amount of work required to produce such wines. Today, the three single vineyard Côte-Rôties owned by Guigal are among the world's most sought-after wines. La Turque, La Mouline, and La Landonne each illustrate a different facet of Côte-Rôtie, according to their specific combination of soil, sub-soil, and slope.

The Côte-Rôtie vineyard contains two famous hills, Côte Blonde and Côte Brune, which produce the best wines of the appellation. Each one takes its name from the nature of its particular soil. In the case of the Côte Blonde, which means "Blond Hill," the soil is dominated by calcereous rock, whereas in the Côte Brune, or

"Brown Hill," the underlying rock is of granite and slate. The local legend in the neighboring town of Ampuis is far more poetic. This tells of the medieval lord of the château, called Seigneur de Maugiron, who had two beautiful daughters, one with blonde hair and the other brown. He accordingly named the twin hills after the color of his daughters' hair. Poetry sometimes gets mixed up with geology.

In the case of Guigal's wines, La Mouline comes from the Côte Blonde, whereas La Landonne and La Turque are both named vineyards of the Côte Brune. Generally softer and more feminine than the Côte Brune, the wines from the Côte Blonde may contain as much as twenty percent of a white grape variety, Viognier, together with Syrah, the unique red grape variety of Côte Rôtie. The wines of the Côte Brune are more tannic and structured, and accordingly require more time to reach maturity. The vineyard of La Turque is

Above: La Turque and its stone-wall terraces.
Below: The vast modern cellar with its lines of oak barrels.

unusual in that it sees the sun all day long, from sunrise to sunset. Most plots are so orientated that they miss either the morning or the evening sun, and their wines will have different character.

The single vineyard approach to Côte-Rôtie has been one of Guigal's innovations. This approach is comparable to that which has been used for Burgundy's greatest wines for some time. The Syrah grape has many different local names in places around the world where it grows. Here in Côte-Rôtie it is known as serine, and is the small-grape variety that produces dark, concentrated wines which can be amongst the longest-lived in the world.

For today's visitor, the house of Guigal shows all the signs of a company undergoing rapid growth. New space has had to be made to harbor all the various activities that surround the making of a wide range of wines from throughout the Rhône Valley, not just from Côte-Rôtie. A guided tour inevitably leads you across pipelines, into rooms full of tanks, and through a maze of cellars and corridors full of barrels. New and old lie cheek by jowl, and, having just left a room full of the latest in wine-making technology, you will be proudly shown the latest

archeological findings of Marcel Guigal. What transpires throughout is a powerful will to make the best wine possible, and, indeed, all the Guigal wines are excellent. The supreme reward for the wine-lover lies at the end of the journey, when you are shown into the tasting cellar where Marcel Guigal, together with his wife and son, regularly taste their wines.

TASTING

◆ La Mouline 1992
As soon as the glass is brought to the nose one can smell the intensity of the wine. The volume and type of aromas form a sphere. The main notes are tobacco, leather, and smokiness. In the mouth, very strong dark berry-fruit flavors explode. The wine's considerable concentration seems lightened by a silky-smooth texture and the lift on the finish. This surely has to do with the presence of white grapes in the blend.

◆ La Turque 1992
This seems younger and sharper on the nose. A rounder, suave feel follows. The mouth feel is absolutely delicious, with a concentration of what seems to be very fresh fruit juices, and a body well-balanced between structure and ripeness. Very rich and long, the final note is velvety.

◆ La Landonne 1992
The nose is so dense one thinks of bitter chocolate. The overall impression is massive and broad shouldered, but never violent. A very concentrated wine that is still closed, it has much more tannins than its cousins, or at least they are far more noticeable. Definitely a wine for the keeping, probably at least twenty years.

A vertical series of La Mouline from 1991, 1990, 1988, 1982, 1978, and 1976 made clear that its qualities include terrific vibrancy and liveliness, with powerful fruit flavors whose characteristics change according to the vintage conditions. Some vintages were fine and delicate, while others, like 1978 and 1990, seemed very firm. To judge from the 1988 La Turque, this wine stays young for a long time, as it still had very youthful and complex fruit flavors, with just a hint of evolution. The term "density" springs to mind when tasting La Landonne. It may not have the elegance of La Mouline, but in time it gains incredible complexity and fullness, and flavors that linger forever on the palate. A wine for patient people.

Château de Beaucastel

It all began in 1309, when Pope Clement V decided to remove himself and his following from Rome to a small region in the south of France known as the Comtat Venaissin, which one of his predecessors had bought some years previously. The pope decided to settle in the main town of the region, Avignon, situated on the northern edge of Provence. This was to remain the capital of the Catholic church until 1377. Although the stay of the popes was brief, compared to their long history, it had considerable repercussions of a more material kind. The successor to Clement V, John XXII, stayed in Avignon and, in 1318, decided to build himself a summer residence in the country nearby. This was to become Châteauneuf-du-Pape, which literally means "the pope's new castle." On the sixty two acres that went with the château, the pope planted olives and vines, and little by little his wine gained itself a fine reputation—probably influenced his position. Neighbors also planted vineyards, following what must have become a fashion. In the early sixteenth century, a Protestant family called Beaucastel bought land at a place known as Coudoulet, near the village of Courthézon. What was initially a barn was transformed into a manor house as their fortune grew, and their arms can still be seen today on the wall of this house that bears their name, as does the famous vineyard which surrounds it.

The story of Châteauneuf-du-Pape is not yet over, as this area was to play a vital part in the establishment of the official French system for regulating the production of fine wines, which has served as an example for many countries since. In the early part of the twentieth century, the owner of another famous property in Châteauneuf, Château Fortia, was a baron Le Roy. In 1923, he set up the bases for what would become, thirteen years later, the appellation contrôlée system. The basic ideas of Baron Le Roy on quality control were quite straightforward. First, the areas allowed to produce fine wines should be controlled and precisely limited, and all fertile soils excluded. In fact, he stipulated that all soils capable of producing thyme or lavender, which are both plants that thrive, like the vine, on poor soils, should be suitable for the Châteauneuf-du-Pape appellation. Second, the grape varieties authorized should be limited and listed. Third, yields should be restricted by mandatory pruning. Fourth, the grapes should be capable of naturally producing at least 12.5 degree alcohol in the finished wine. Grapes had to be sorted at harvest, and at least five percent discarded to avoid rotten or poor quality grapes being used in the wine-making process. Rosé wine, considered by Le Roy to be of second order, was banned in Châteauneuf. Finally, every wine had to pass the test of a tasting panel who would decide whether it was worthy of bearing the name Châteauneuf-du-Pape.

Give or take a few modifications, this legislation still holds, which probably proves that it was well-born. However, the citizens of Châteauneuf remained extremely wary of the dangers of any outside influences that might adversely affect the quality of their

Opposite: The vineyard at Beaucastel is full of the stones rolled down by the river Rhône, and mixed with sand and clay.
Above: The Château de Beaucastel is an oasis of shade and cool.

wines, as the town council published an order in 1954 which quite seriously forbid "flying machines of any description, whether saucer-shaped or cigar-shaped" to fly over the territory of Châteauneuf, "whatever their nationality." They had an afterthought for forced landings, as they also stipulated that "any machine caught landing on the territory would immediately be impounded." History does not reveal whether the council's deliberations took place before or after the annual wine-tasting!

The soil of this vineyard is a result of a long process of grinding carried out by the Rhône over thousands of years. From its sources in the Alpine glaciers to the Camargue delta, just south of Avignon, the river carries huge quantities of stones and rocks which, through being rolled against one another by the river, become smooth pebbles and are mixed with sand and clay. These layers of apparently inhospitable soil are in fact the starting point for the richness of Châteauneuf. The Perrin family, who own Beaucastel, fully respect the true nature of this soil, as they consider it to be an integral part of the quality of their wine. They are accordingly very careful about any substance that may alter its composition. Chemical product whose long-term

effects are unknown are out, and natural products are in, albeit in limited quantities. The ecosystem of the vine plant has to be understood in all its aspects and with all its ramifications. Is the taste of a wild strawberry comparable

to the taste of one that has been raised under a plastic tunnel, fed on synthetic fertilizers? The same goes for grapes, whether they are made into wine or not. A wine of character requires grapes of character.

Above: Old vines in Châteauneuf vineyards whitened by stones.
Right: Traditional hogsheads at Beaucastel.
Below: The house at Beaucastel started life as a barn, in the sixteenth century.

For the wine-lover, the list of the thirteen authorized grape varieties of Châteauneuf-du-Pape is full of poetry, and evokes the gravelly sounds of the local Provençal accent. The names just roll off the tongue like the stones of the vineyards: Grenache, Mourvèdre, Syrah, Cinsault, Counoise, Vaccarèse, Terret Noir, Muscardin, Clairette, Picpoul, Picardin, Roussanne, and Bourboulenc. That makes eight red varieties and five whites. Beaucastel is one of the rare Chateauneuf estates to use every one of them, and each one is made separately and tasted before deciding on the final blend. François Perrin considers that a great wine is above all a "noble wine," by which he means the product of a symbiosis between unadulterated soils, a well-adapted range of grape varieties, and a suitable climate.

Beaucastel's objective has always been to make a wine of strong personality, which will reveal different aspects of its character through time. The multiple facets of the soil, the climate, and the grape varieties should all be a part of this, as should the wine-maker, whose job is to reconcile short-term and long-term, as such wines may be drunk within a few years or after a generation. Beaucastel's red wines are made to last well over ten years, and therefore age slowly. In a case like this, the long-term vision necessary for the production of such a wine has little or nothing to do with any usual financial logic. Total commitment is the term, and this requires a profound fascination for the mystery of wine. Trying to understand and striving for excellence are what drives this commitment. François Perrin is convinced that such passion should show in any wine made by someone who has given his utmost to make it. When asked which vintages of Beaucastel are his favorites, he immediately talks of those made by his father or grandfather. In qualifying the way some of these very old wines taste today, he talks of "grape jam," which describes their extreme concentration and fruit. Wine is a messenger that can travel through time.

Tasting

White wine

◆ *Beaucastel blanc vieilles vignes 1992*
The nose of this wine is filled with some very powerful aromas that are difficult to name. The complexity in the mouth is equal to the nose. It is particularly hard to put an age on this wine, as it seems neither young nor old. The texture and aromas are filling and give the wine exceptional length.

Red wines

◆ *Beaucastel 1994 (still in hogshead)*
Closed in to begin with, the nose opens with an animal-like smell, followed by concentrated berry fruit and spices to follow. The mouth feel is full and soft, packed with fruit. The power is latent and comes on progressively.

◆ *Beaucastel 1990*
The nose is more concentrated, but remains fresh and lively. After a few minutes in the glass, a wide range of aromas come out: wood, fruit, and some more earthy, mineral smells. In the mouth, the wine is pure and very powerful. Its tannins are strong but never overpowering.

◆ *Beaucastel 1986*
This wine has covered the time span usually necessary for Beaucastel to reach maturity. More evolved the nose offers powerful aromas, which recall game and a touch of jam. The mouth feel is strong, with excellent fruit and fine tannins that last. The aftertaste is delightfully fresh.

◆ *Beaucastel 1976*
Another ten years on, and one is struck by the continuity of the aromas that were there in the 1986: principally game and jam. In the mouth, the difference is more striking, as the wine has rounded out, rather like someone whose once-broad shoulders now have a slight slope to them. The wine is still powerful, but with a softer edge and a wonderfully long follow-through.

◆ *Beaucastel 1970*
Could this be the ideal age for a great vintage of Beaucastel? The nose carries on that animal touch, with a lift which lightens it, and all kinds of fruit in jam. The mouth has an extraordinary feel to it: fruit and tannins play together in a silky dance that alternates strength and softness, sweetness and freshness.
For a second or two the wine seems sweet, but then that impression fades.
Fruit and tannins have metamorphosed into a sort of eternal grape juice.

Mas de Daumas Gassac

In most parts of Europe where the climate is considered capable of bearing vineyards, man has tried planting them at some point in time. Many people assume from this that there is no further potential for the creation of great wines in the Old World beyond those that have existed for a long time. Continuity in wine-making in the traditional production areas for fine wines is considered, in some mysterious way, as proof that only such areas are capable of producing great wines. This is absurd, as a number of recent examples have shown. Given suitable soil and climate factors, and the vital ingredient of human endeavor, several enterprising growers have proved that it is perfectly possible to create a wine of top quality from a site that was previously unknown. Some Italian entrepreneurs have succeeded, as well as Spanish and French. Aimé Guibert is one such man. The story of Mas de Daumas Gassac is particularly remarkable in a country whose wine-makers have too often taken refuge behind a mass of legislation that combines protectionism with insufficiency, rather than bravely seeking out the true conditions that enable a great wine to be made.

Although it respects, in some ways, the very old wine-making traditions of its Languedoc area, Mas de Daumas Gassac has succeeded, in the space of one generation, in creating a top wine estate from nothing, just as many have done in New World countries. As with every success story, good luck played its part. When Aimé and Véronique Guibert de la Vayssière bought a farm

Above: The house, whose original exterior has been preserved.
Above right: Peach trees blossom alongside the still bare vines as spring arrives.
Right: A cross-section of the special soil that played such a large part in the birth of this wine.

near the town of Montpellier from the Daumas family in the early 1970's, they had no plans to concentrate on making wine. Among the crops that they considered planting on the property to make it pay its way were corn, olives, and grape vines. To go about things properly, knowing little themselves, they called on the help of specialists. One of these, an eminent professor of geography and geology named Henri Enjalbert, was to play a crucial role in the course of events. As he wandered around the estate to size it up, he noticed some extremely deep layers of fine red soil where an access road had just been cut through the hillside. On first sight, he declared that this was probably glacial in its origins and that it reminded him of parts of Burgundy's Côte d'Or. After an analysis of samples, Professor Enjalbert told the Guiberts that this soil constituted a sort of "geological miracle," and that in his opinion, given the relatively cool meso-climate that prevails in the Gassac Valley, the estate had the potential to produce a truly great wine, on a level with the best from Bordeaux or Burgundy.

Almost twenty-five years later his hunch has been proved right: there is now the

Below: The estate is named after the Gassac stream which runs through it.

equivalent of a "Grand Cru" in the Languedoc, and there will probably be others. The wines of Daumas Gassac, at first red and now also white, continue to surprise tasters from around the world. A continuous process of exploring the possibilities of Gassac's "terroir" has been going on since then. The first plantings were mainly of Bordeaux's grape varieties, with a clearly defined aim to make a fine red wine. Since then, as the land has gradually been cleared, some plots have been deemed more suitable for white grapes. To take his exploration as far as possible, Aimé Guibert has tried all kinds of grape varieties at Daumas Gassac: Cabernet Sauvignon, Merlot, Malbec, Cabernet Franc, Tannat, Syrah, Pinot Noir, Nebbiolo, Dolcetto, and Barbera, and that is just the reds. The collection of white varieties is even more impressive and includes Viognier, Petit Manseng, Marsanne, Roussanne, Chardonnay, Chenin Blanc, and Bourboulenc, all from France, with Petite Arvigne and Amigne, from Switzerland, and Sercial from Madeira. There are even a few plants of a virtually unknown variety from Yemen, of the Lebanese Datta, and of the mythical Neherlescol from Israël. According to the Bible, this variety was capable of producing bunches that were so big that they required two men to carry them. Known to the Babylonians five thousand years ago, there is exactly 0.1 percent of this grape blended into the white wine of Daumas Gassac.

Farming techniques are exclusively organic and quite traditional at Mas de Daumas Gassac, so no pesticides, chemical weed-killers, or chemical fertilizers are used. The landscape has its part to play, not only in the beauty of the scenery, but also in the general ecosystem, so many fields and scrub or woodland areas have been left deliberately between the vineyards. The sheltering function of tree belts is well-known, but it may be that the many wild herbs in the "garrigue," or scrubland, also impart some of their aromas to the wine.

TASTING

◆ *1985*
The color is very dark and seems hardly to have evolved over ten years. The nose is rich and very concentrated and contains a wide range of fruit aromas, like cassis, as well as tobacco and game, as a sign of aging. The mouth can feel the tannins, but they are lightened by the fresh-feeling fruit. This is a muscular wine, still a bit wild but not overpowering, which needs another ten years to reach its best.

Domaine Huet

This part of the the Loire Valley is known as "the garden of France," and the name suits it very well. The landscapes, the light, and the climate are filled with a softness and calm that make it as restful as a garden. Wine was first made here around the fourth century, when the first monasteries were established. Upstream from Tours, on the right bank of the Loire River, Vouvray was the site of the abbey of Marmoutier which was founded by Saint Martin in 372. For centuries, France's kings used this region as their main playground for various hedonistic activities: art, hunting, gastronomy, and, of course, love. This was the region that gave birth to the French way of life. One of its most celebrated poets, the eccentric and exuberant Rabelais, came from Chinon, which is not far from Vouvray. He was particularly inspired by life in the Loire Valley and was one of the most ardent upholders of the principle that the pleasures of wine and food, and their harmonies, were the best way of unifying mind and matter. Having been both monk and doctor probably gave him added credibility for his ideas. In any event, he was totally convinced that good food and good wine, in considerable quantities, were far better for one's health than dieting and abstinence.

Founded in 1928, the Huet estate at Vouvray owns seventy nine acres of vineyards nowadays. Nearby lie the banks of the Loire, which have been gradually shaped over the centuries by this great river. This process of erosion has created a series of pockets of soil, of varying depths and nature, set into the limestone subsoil. These natural conditions have been used to their advantage by Huet, as they provide the potential for several different wines. Three of the wines in their range are named after specific vineyard plots: le

Above: Troglodytic dwellings in the limestone cliffs at Vouvray.

Above: The Haut-Lieu vineyard in the morning's mist during winter. Opposite: The cellars are dug out of the limestone and provide perfect storage temperatures for the wines.

Haut-Lieu, Le Mont, and Le Bourg. As for the grape variety, Vouvray produces only white wines, of varying levels of dryness or sweetness, from a single grape variety, the Chenin Blanc. This will naturally accentuate the capacity of the various vineyard plots to differentiate their wines, rather like in Burgundy. Apart from differences due to soil, the warmer years will produce more sugar in the grapes, making it possible to make semi-sweet or, in exceptional years, sweet wines, in addition to dry.

All this makes it perfectly clear that there can be no question of making a standardized wine, unvariably the same in its taste from one vintage to another, at

Domaine Huet. Listening to Noël Pinguet, the estate's managing director, as he explains his wine-making philosophy is a lesson in modesty and clarity, although the phenomena involved are far from simple. "The wine-maker is at the grape's service, and not the other way around. A great wine almost makes itself; one helps it on its way, but one cannot rectify it." Logically, the agricultural methods used on the estate respect nature. It is the distinct individual character of each wine produced by Huet that makes the production so sincerely fine. According to the weather conditions in a given year, certain plots will produce more grape sugar than others. If the autumn is fine, they will risk harvesting a little later to let the natural sugar build up in the bunches. In fact, each of the three vineyards could, in theory, produce three different wines each year: dry, demi-sec, and moelleux, or sweet.

Vouvray wines can last for at least thirty or forty years. The exceptional vintages for Noël Pinguet have been 1947, 1959, 1989, and 1990, and these wines are set to last much longer. This aging capacity is due to a perfect balance between the wine's strong acidity and its other substances, which also enables it to resist exposure to oxygen when the bottle has been opened. One can drink just a glass from a bottle of Vouvray, and, replacing the cork, leave the bottle in a cool place until the following day. The wine will not have lost its aromas; on the contrary, there is every chance that it will have developed more of them. The beneficial effect of air on wines of this type is a constant source of interest and explains why it is often advisable to pour young wines of this level into a decanter before serving. White wines will benefit from this as much as red wines, but the capacity to constantly release new aromas, over a period of several hours, is one of the signs of a great wine.

TASTING

◆ *Cuvée Constance 1995*
This wine is a blend between wines from the three individual vineyards. It has a deep color for a young Vouvray, which is usually greenish-tinged. The nose is highly complex and reminds one of linden flowers, sherry, and wood, below a layer of honey. Despite its richness, the fruit is as delicate as lace. The overall impression is smooth, fresh, and very harmonious.

Coulée de Serrant

There are times when one is tempted to link the nature of light found in a particular place with the nature of the wine it produces. Down river from the town of Angers, where the Loire River begins to pick up speed towards the Atlantic Ocean, the light that surrounds the valley blends the silvery brilliance of the sea with the soft translucency of the surrounding countryside. On the banks of the Loire, precisely at the point where the "coulée," or stream, of Serrant flows into the main river, two stone obelisks rise from the ground as if to indicate to the passerby a special significance of the place.

The vineyards of Coulée de Serrant produce a rare wine that manages to taste both crisp and gentle, powerful and delicate. Perhaps one could attribute this unusual capacity to reconcile opposites to a special osmosis that operates, close to water, between air, water, and earth. This is converted in the wine into a series of notes that alternate lightness, strength, and mineral elements, which serve to remind one of the complexity of the plant's environment. In the vineyard, the plots are angled either towards the Loire River or towards the small valley of the Coulée. In some parts, the ground is so steep that no tractor can be used to cultivate it. Each facet of this vineyard catches a different angle of the sun's rays, which will transform the substances in the plant in a particular way. Like the river down below, which slowly digs its way into soil and rock, the vine twists and turns to send its roots into the shale rock, forming those knotty shapes that show the contrasting influences that nature has brought to bear.

Opposite: Rows of vines curve over the hillside before diving towards the Loire River.
Above: The old priory at Coulée de Serrant, which is the home of Nicolas Joly.

Although it is usually risky to put a precise date to the founding of ancient vineyards, it is more than likely that the first plantings at Coulée de Serrant go back to the twelfth century and were made by the monks of the abbey of Saint Nicholas d'Angers. This is borne out by the presence of a neighboring vineyard called La Roche aux Moines, which means "the monk's rock," and where there have been vines for over six centuries. Both these vineyards are within the commune of Savennières and have the status of Grand Cru. The Coulée de Serrant vineyards cover seventeen acres, divided into three separate plots: le Grand Clos, les Plantes, and le Clos du Château, each with its specific angle and slope. Only one grape variety is allowed here, the Chenin Blanc, which also goes by the local name of Pineau de Loire. Its naturally fresh and lively flavors are sometimes amplified, sometimes modified by the different soils and meso-climate in the various vineyards. Walking through them makes one very aware of the nature of this ground. The slope is often very steep, and the jagged shale rocks that point upwards are treacherous underfoot but enable the rain to penetrate deep to the roots. Coulée de Serrant is considered so specific as a vineyard that it is an appellation in its own right, like Château-Grillet in the Rhône Valley.

The Joly family own Coulée de Serrant, and Nicolas Joly manages the estate. He is a firm believer in the specific identity of "terroir," as the beginning of everything in a wine. What makes a wine unique is the synthesis that takes place at a given time between the plant, the soil, and the environment. For the past fifteen years, he has applied what are known as biodynamic natural farming techniques

to the estate and will take as much pride in showing one his cows as the vineyard. This stems from a global attitude to life and nature that takes into account the interactions between all its parts and is concerned with the balance between the

Opposite (upper): The château of la Roche aux Moines, which takes its name from the monks of a former monastery.
Opposite (lower): In the library.
Above: Wild flowers are encouraged in the vineyards.
Below: One of the world's greatest white wines is made in this cellar.

elements rather than an isolated vision of just one of them. The biodynamic approach regards the earth as living matter, on account of the microorganisms that are an essential part of it. This approach leads to developing a plant's natural resistance to all forms of disease. Nicolas Joly will not claim that a good wine can be produced simply by applying such methods. What is more important is that this approach implies a constant and wide-ranging observation of nature that inevitably leads the wine-maker to try to understand the causes behind phenomena. It is the antithesis of an industrial approach, which leads to standardization. The implications are high commitment levels and a long-term view of things, as life cycles can be very long.

TASTING

It is best to keep Coulée de Serrant for about fifteen years before drinking, in order to let its extraordinarily complex aromas develop. Unlike simpler white wines, service temperature should not be too fresh. Ideal cellar temperature (around 14°C, or 55°F) is perfect.

◆ *Coulée de Serrant 1994*
The nose, although still closed-in, is reminiscent of dried fruit, honey, and linden-flower. The mouth is fresh and opulent and goes through a fascinating series of dry and semi-dry sensations that caress the palate. The crispness has been dissolved into the richer substance of the wine, making it seem intense without being over-rich. This is a beautifully subtle wine.

◆ *Coulée de Serrant 1976*
The color is very bright, of an amber-gold hue. The nose gives off a vast range of aromas, both vegetable and mineral. Oxygen has slowly worked on the wine to

calm its youthful ardor, liberating notes of orange peel and something reminiscent of the smell of stones under a hot sun.
There is no need to chill this wine to give it freshness: when tasted at 17°C (62° F), its strong, smooth acidity gave a delicious lift to its silky texture. The aromas are incredibly persistent in the mouth, mixing fruit and mineral elements that vibrate together on the palate.

Sassicaia

At the end of the Second World War, an Italian connoisseur of Bordeaux's great wines, Marchese Mario Incisa della Rocchetta, moved his family to a property thirty one miles south of the town of Livorno, facing the Mediterranean sea. This was not the easiest time to find his favorite wines, and the local production was not up to the demands of a discerning palate, so the marquis decided that he would produce his own wine. To start with, he used some French grafts of Cabernet Sauvignon that he managed to obtain from Château Lafite. The fact that this was to be the birth of a truly great growth in Italy would actually take quite a few years to emerge. The marquis' friends who tasted the first vintages from the initial vineyard plot of 3.7 acres at San Guido decided that the wine was undrinkable! This may have had as much to do with its unusual taste compared to local wines as with the fairly primitive wine-making techniques used at that time. Nobody knows the real reason for sure, but the friends definitely didn't like the wine. Even after having refined his wine-making techniques, the marquis always refused to sell any of his wine, as his sole ambition had always been to supply his own cellar. So, for fifteen years, the only people to taste the wine from the San Guido estate were family and close friends. It seems clear that the friends gradually took to the wine, for when Mario's son, Niccolo, became involved in the family estate, he managed to persuade his father to sell some of the wine in order to satisfy the demand of a small circle of amateurs. A star had been born, almost by accident.

Opposite: The first vineyard plot to be planted on the San Guido estate, in a valley high up behind the Château de Castglioncello. Above: The alley of cypress trees, three miles long, that was planted by the current owner's great-grandmother.

The first vintage to be marketed was the 1968. By then, the vineyard area had grown to include a plot called "Sassicaia," which means "stony place." This area was gave name to the wine of Tenuta San Guido and became a symbol of the creative capacity that Italy's wine-makers showed in the 1970's and 1980's. Sassicaia was the first Italian wine to prove that it could be judged on a par with the best from France. One of the earliest tests was an international tasting held in London in 1978 by Hugh Johnson, at which the 1975 Sassicaia was judged to be the best wine produced from the Cabernet Sauvignon grape. Since then, customers the world over have been struggling to buy cases of this great wine. Although he was fundamentally opposed to selling his wine on the market, fearing that this would lead to its taste becoming standardized, the Marchese Mario Incisa's intuition as to the potential of his vineyard proved to be right. His son, Niccolo, believes that a great wine is essentially made in the vineyard. One is tempted to ask why it took until the latter half of the twentieth century to discover the wine-making potential of an area which has been inhabited for several millennia, in a country covered with vines for two thousand years. The reason probably lies with the recurring difficulties that local inhabitants had, over the centuries, in settling on this part of the Italian coast. The coastal area was, until quite recently, particularly inhospitable through swamps and the accompanying hordes of mosquitoes. Pirates coming from the sea made it perilous to plant anything more than annual crops, and the population frequently had to flee to the mountains and dense forests inland. The old fortified castle of Castiglioncello that overlooks the vineyard serves as a reminder of these troubled times. The meso-climate here is particularly favorable, as can be judged from the terrible winter of 1985, which killed about eighty percent of Tuscany's extensive olive groves yet spared those planted on the hills facing the sea.

One of the pleasures of a wine-lover looking for wines that will keep is to be able to enjoy a bottle of Sassicaia at any stage of its life. This may well explain why it is very difficult to find any at wine auctions, otherwise a happy hunting ground for older wines. This "drinkability" of young vintages of Sassicaia is one of the objectives of its wine-makers. Pleasure being the goal, when tasting in the beautifully simple cellar of Tenuta San Guido with the Marchese Niccolo, there is no point in trying to find complicated aromas in the wine or in some corner of one's imagination. The key issue is whether it

Opposite: The bell-tower of the chapel of Castiglioncello, which overlooks the oldest vineyards of Sassicaia.
Above: The estate buildings of San Guido, home to Sassicaia.

Sassicaia at table

The strong personality of a great wine enables it to go with a wide range of dishes. Why not play with local traditions and serve the recipe of the Marchese Mario Inchisa for polenta, together with squab in its blood sauce, as at the Gambero Rosso, that wonderful restaurant on the coast. A taste of paradise.

tastes good. For someone whose great-grandmother planted a double row of cypress trees three miles long just to get access to the village of Bolgheri, there is no point beating about the bush! Legendary wines inevitably generate myths . One day, the local police found a hitchhiker wandering along the highway, exhausted and without a lira in his pocket. The only word they could get out of him that made any sense to them was: Sassicaia! And who can beat the enthusiasm of those amateurs from Montreal who, having forged their team spirit by waiting for hours in subzero temperatures just to have the privilege of reserving a case or two of the precious nectar when the futures release hit the local wine store, formed a club whose motto is: "I froze my ass to get my sass!"

TASTING

Just one wine is made at Sassicaia. It spends around two years in oak barrels before being delivered to markets.

♦ *1988*
Deliciously expressive fruit, with a silky texture. Plenty of lift and structure. Lovely clean finish. A wine of class that shows just how refined Cabernets can be.

♦ *1985*
A very full and concentrated wine, with considerably more power than the 1988, this wine is only just beginning to round. Absolutely magnificent now, it has the capacity to wait for a long time.

Bruno Giacosa

When the Greeks first reached the Italian peninsula in the seventh century B.C., they found vines so widely planted that they called the country Oenotria, or "land of vines." Nowadays, Italy is the biggest single producer of wine in the world, although this has not always been the case throughout the centuries. There are vineyards in every province of Italy, from north to south, and the "denominazione di origine"(DO) system that was installed in 1963, following that of France, reflects the spread and diversity of the production. In the northwest corner of the country, near the French border, the province of Piedmont is the perfect illustration of this complexity, with more than forty authorized production areas, a record for Italy. Here, in the region of Alba, also famous for its white truffles and its mushrooms, are two of the oldest and most famous of the delimited areas. What is more, they have the highest possible ranking in the system's hierarchy: Barolo and Barbaresco are both Denominazione di Origine Controllata e Garantita (DOCG). In these twin areas on either side of the town of Alba, wine-makers have pioneered a drive for top quality in Italian wines over the past thirty years. Climate and grape variety are identical, and there only being a few miles between them, the differences in the style of Barolo compared to that of Barbaresco is very much a question of nuances and has a lot to do with individual wine-making styles. One could say, however, that in general Barolo tends to be more austere in its youth and, therefore, has a longer

Opposite: Bruno Giacosa's Faletto estate, with the village of Serralunga in the background.
Above: Stainless steel fermenting tanks in the impeccably clean winery.

life expectancy. There is no doubt that both possess strong personalities, but how can one define these personalities?

To answer this question, one must look closely at all the ingredients. To start with, there is the unique red grape variety, Nebbiolo. For a traveler on the roads of northern Italy, this word will probably be familiar, as "nebbia" means fog, and the road signs are full of warnings against this danger. Just as capricious as the weather condition, the Nebbiolo, like the Pinot Noir, is notoriously difficult to cultivate. Until the mid-nineteenth century, Nebbiolo was used mainly for the production of sweet red wines. Count Cavour, who along with Napoleon III of France, was the guiding hand behind the unification of Italy, was to change that. Cavour's family property was in the region of Alba, and he gradually shifted wine production from sweet red to dry red. As a long-standing admirer of France and its great wines, he saw the future in the production of fine dry red wines destined for long cellaring. He therefore hired a Frenchman named Louis Oudart as cellar-master and entrusted him with the mission of explaining the new ideas to the grape-growers. A century later, the results were clear, and Barolo and Barbaresco were both given DOCG status in 1963. Shortly afterwards, in the 1970's, modern wine-making techniques provided the conditions for a second revolution. Better understanding enabled wine-makers to exert more control over the process. But this is not to diminish the unique thing about the Langhe hills region around Alba: its "terroir" is made up of calcareous rock and hillside vineyards, which give great diversity of slope, sun angle, and altitude. The Alps add spectacular beauty to the backdrop behind medieval villages set on the crest of the hills.

The village of Neive is typical of the region's history. The approach to the village is by a steep road that climbs between vineyards which cover the hill. The old village still has its cobbled streets, bell towers and the remains of a former château. The modern village is at the bottom of the hill, spread out along the busy road. Here is the functional and impeccably clean winery of Bruno Giacosa, whose family has been making wine for three generations. The facade of the buildings is modest, exactly like their owner, who clearly considers that his wine is the key issue, not the trappings. Giacosa gives a simple order to the relative importance of the elements of a fine wine: first of all, the grapes; second,

the wine-making; finally, the aging process. In his opinion, words are inadequate to describe a great wine, and he leaves long discussions on the relative merits of each wine to others, just nodding his head to signify agreement with some of the commentaries.

As to the making of his Barolos and Barbarescos, Bruno Giacosa is an ardent defender of the traditional approach, and he uses wooden hogsheads to mature his red wines. The impeccably clean winery,

with its stainless steel fermenting tanks, shows, however, that many of the lessons of modern wine-making have not been lost around here. Bruna, his daughter, looks after the commercial aspect of the winery with boundless energy, greatly contributing to spreading the reputation of its wines, of which sixty percent are currently exported. Her main difficulty consists in keeping the many connoisseurs of Giacosa's wines happy with just a third of the production that normal demand requires! This production is divided between several types of wine and a series of appellations. The best known are the Barolos and Barbarescos, mainly from single vineyards as in Burgundy's top wines, but Giacosa also makes what is widely regarded as one of Italy's best sparkling wines, a spumante from the Pinot Noir grape. Owner of a fine vineyard estate in Barolo, near the village of Serralunga d'Alba, Giacosa also buys grapes from neighboring vine-growers to make his wines.

Opposite: One of the bell towers in the village of Neive.
Below: The beauty of life in the Piedmont, with the Alps in the background.

TASTING

The great vintages for Barolo and Barbaresco are 1961, 1964, 1967, 1971, 1978, 1982, 1985, 1988, 1989, and 1990. To continue this list one will have to wait a while, as the wines must age for at least three years before being granted their appellation.

♦ Barbaresco Asili 1990
From Giacosa's own vineyard, this wine is quite extraordinary. It is hard to compare the nose to anything else, with the possible exception of some older burgundies. There are many fruit aromas, both from red and black fruit, with a strong reminder of prunes. This first nose makes the wine seem very young, but the next wave is like that of a much older wine, full of animal and truffle smells. The mouth feel has supple tannins and fine, intense fruit flavors, both light and earthy. The Nebbiolo grape shows both depth and finesse.

♦ Barolo Faletto 1990
Here is a demonstration of the harmony and complexity that can be achieved in great Barolos.

The density has an almost animal-like feel to it, with an elegantly smoky touch. The mouth is even fuller, and excellent fruit flavors balance and surround the strong tannins. Although the wine is long and powerful, it never loses the distinctive, lifting freshness of the wines from this area—the proof that Barolo can reconcile sensations which are usually opposed.

Gaja

The history of wine has its alternate cycles, like the vine plant. Short revolutionary periods, which produce long-lasting changes, alternate with longer periods where continuity, introspection, and rest are the rule. Anglo Gaja is definitely someone who contributed to setting off one of the periods of change in Italy. Since he started working in the family business in the 1960's, innovations have kept coming. The list is convincing enough: improvements to vine trellising and pruning, the decision to make and sell wines from his own vineyards only, single vineyard wines, modifications to traditional wine-making techniques, positioning of his wines on a level with the best from France, creation of an Italian distribution company that handles a remarkable selection of some of the best wines in the world, planting French grape varieties, regular purchases of some of the finest plots of vineyard in the area, and, recently, the acquisition of the Castello of Barbaresco, right across the road from the Gaja cellars and offices. To make a long story short, Angelo Gaja, together with a handful of other inventive and ambitious wine-makers, has put the concept of great wine on the map in a country which, until fairly recently, had generally considered, and indeed still does, in the case of some trattorias, that there were only two categories of wine: "bianco" and "rosso" !

The Gaja family came from Spain to the Piedmont in the eighteenth century. Angelo Gaja's great-grandfather founded the estate in 1859. The vineyard now covers about 198 acres and is the sole source of grapes for Gaja wines. The range of wines produced follows a double rationale: first of all the traditional grape varieties and appellations of the area, in particular Barolo, Barbaresco, and Alba; then a minority share of about fifteen

Above: Traditional hogsheads cohabit with new oak barrels and stainless steel tanks, in other parts of the winery.

**Above (upper): The gentle rise and fall of the Langhe hills shows a small parcel of Gaja's vineyards in Barbaresco.
Above (lower):
A hidden treasure of old vintages, discovered during recent enlargements of the cellars.**

percent given over to the experimental production of French grape varieties, which naturally fall outside the DOC system. In the small village of Barbaresco, one can spend any length of time hunting for a sign directing visitors to this winery, which exports about eighty percent of its production to those who seek excellence with a degree of innovation in their wines. A large metal door, discreetely

afternoon, Robert Mondavi repeated his question a third time, and Gaja, surprised and intrigued, asked the meaning of this joke. Mondavi just answered: "Can't you hear it? People here are snoring in their sleep, day and night." This little lesson on the unexploited potential of this region did not fall on deaf ears.

Along with his taste for innovation, Gaja clearly has a deeply-felt attachment to his own family tradition and to this part of Piedmont. This shows up in the frequent use of words from the local dialect or references to family history to describe many of his wines. For example, he calls his wine made from Cabernet Sauvignon "Darmagi," which means "what a pity" in Piedmontese. The origin is that every time he went past this particular vineyard which Angelo had planted to Cabernet, having pulled out the Nebbiolo, his father uttered this word with a sorrowful shake of his head. This ability to integrate everything available to give specific identity to wines, whether the elements be technical or poetical, learned or instinctively felt, is a sure sign of an open and eclectic mind.

painted dark green, is the only external indication of a totally functional, five-story winery, topped by a beautiful paved courtyard and some extremely elegant offices. Unlike many wine-growing areas around the world, cellar-door sales are not the thing here; as in Italy, local specialist wine shops still play a vital part in the distribution of wines. The aesthetics of the Gaja labels are also very distinctive, graphically strong and yet sober. The powerful alliance between tradition and modernity is immediately apparent.

There are stories that tell as much about the great personalities of the world of wine as pages of explanations. In 1973, Gaja had a visit from Robert Mondavi. After a tour around the local vineyards, Mondavi asked Gaja whether he could hear a noise in the air. The day was peaceful and Gaja could pick out nothing in particular, so Mondavi just said: "Oh well, I must be mistaken then." The same scene was repeated on the terrace of the restaurant, at lunch. At the end of the

TASTING

◆ *Barbaresco Sori San Lorenzo 1990*
The quality of both the 1991 and the 1992 harvests were considered insufficient to produce a vintage wine. San Lorenzo is the patron saint of the town of Alba. The nose of this wine is wonderfully deep and elegant. Fleshy in the mouth, it rapidly reveals some vigorous young tannins. But there is plenty of material to soften their impact. The wine is young and densely knit, but harmonious with a clean finish.

◆ *Barolo Sperss 1991*
Up to 1961, Gaja produced Barolo made from brought-in grapes. The decision to make only wines from their own vineyards implied that Gaja had to give up making

Barolo, Piedmont's most prestigious wine, until the opportunity arose to buy a fine vineyard near Serralunga. When the wine was finally made, Gaja decided to name it Sperss, which means "nostalgia" in Piedmontese.
The nose is very fine, both elegant and intense. The fruit has kept all its youthful freshness in the mouth, lifted by the acidity. The tannins make the wine long without becoming aggressive. A fine, classy wine with considerable power.

Bodegas Vega-Sicilia

In Old Castile, Valladolid reached its peak in the seventeenth century when it was the capital of Spain. Then it slipped into relative oblivion, and its past glory had little or no influence on the renown of Spain's greatest wine, Vega-Sicilia, whose vineyards date from the 1860's. There is naturally a long wine-making tradition in this Duero Valley, as in so many other parts of Europe where the climate makes it possible to ripen grapes, but the reputation of its wines had never traveled beyond the regional boundaries. Until the arrival of railways, the main towns of the province of Castille y Léon—Burgos, Salamanca, and Valladolid—provided sufficient outlets for the local wine, and there was little motivation to increase production at a time when transport was so difficult. The Duero River, which flows from Spain to Portugal, where it becomes the Douro, is not navigable in its upper reaches, and even if it had been, the incessant wars between the two nations of the Iberic peninsula would have prevented access to the Atlantic Ocean and the shipping routes to the expanding markets of northern Europe in the seventeenth and eighteenth centuries.

Traveling into Spain from Portugal by road enables one to see how radically the landscape changes between the spectacular slopes of the upper Douro in Portugal, where the greatest port grapes are grown, and the area of Ribera del Duero near Valladolid. The wild mountainous country on the Portuguese side gives way to a broader, flatter landscape with rich pastures crossed by streams, overlooked by the occasional rocky bluff. The towns passed bring back memories from history: Cuidad Rodrigo, Salamanca,

Burgos—all strongholds of past battles. The main crops are wheat and grass, for this is a region that breeds some of Spain's fighting bulls. While the vegetation is dense and varied on the Portuguese side of the border, here trees are rarer and confined to either oak or pine. These somewhat austere vistas are typical of Castile, and continue to the east of Valladolid and the town of Soria, where one begins to see the result of the Duero's passage through the limestone hills. This magnificent landscape, which seems to step from a watercolor painting, was perfectly described by the Spanish poet Antonio Machado, "Silver hills, gray slopes, purple rocks, between which the Duero draws the bow-line of its curve."

In the month of April, it is striking to witness how much later spring comes to these high plains of Spain than to the sheltered slopes of the Douro Valley, westwards and lower down, in Portugal. The combined influence of the Atlantic Ocean and the lower altitude means that bud-burst, when the vines first show shoots of green, comes three or four weeks earlier for the Port vineyards than for those of Ribera del Duero. Up on these continental plains, temperature variations between winter and summer are so extreme that a local saying describes the climate thus: "Nine months of winter, three months of hell." Such extremes obviously have an influence on the way the grapes ripen. Suffice it to say that, after a late start, it all happens very fast. On a mainly limestone soil similar to that of Burgundy, the grape varieties planted at Vega-Sicilia form an unusual combination. The local red grape, Tempranillo, is the dominant

Opposite: Old Tempranillo vines, bush pruned, waiting for spring to come.
Above: After maturing in wood, Vega-Sicilia's wines further age in bottles
before being deemed ready for delivery to customers.

partner, with sixty percent. Although little known outside of Spain, it has great capabilities. The founder of Vega-Sicilia, impressed with the top wines from Bordeaux, also planted the Bordeaux varieties Cabernet Sauvignon, Merlot, and Malbec. Don Eloy Lecanda y Chaves was not afraid of innovation. Until 1864, the farm, or finca, that he bought had belonged to a family called Santos Sicilia, and Vega is the name of the valley in which the vineyards lie.

Bodegas Vega-Sicilia has changed hands several times since then, but never has wine-making been the mainstay of its owners' activities. This has probably enabled each successive proprietor to pamper Vega-Sicilia as a spoiled child who should never want for anything. Their will has never wavered: to create, at Vega-Sicilia, the reference in Spain for a great wine. Today, the wine is clearly one of the world's greatest, proudly different

Above: The castle of Queen Joan of Castile, known as Mad Joan.
Below: The buildings impress with their size and their sober facades.
Opposite: To control the all-important aging of its wines, Vega-Sicilia has its own cooperage. Here oak staves weather prior to being made into barrels.

as befits the Spanish character. One illustration of this is its unusual sales technique, which would be the envy of many a commercial director in other fields. To be able to buy a case of Vega-Sicilia in Spain, you have first to be accepted on a list of potential buyers. After a few years, depending on your luck, or maybe on how influential you or your friends are, you will receive a letter authorizing you to reserve a case or two of the precious wine, to be

delivered only when the cellar-master decides that it is ready. Woe betide you if you decline the offer, as you will probably not be given another opportunity!

Visiting the estate with Mariano Garcia, the manager and cellar-master, is quite an experience. One soon learns how unique and comprehensive the Vega-Sicila policy is for aging their wines. The bodega is almost as well-guarded as a military base, and the buildings are impressive for their size and the sober beauty of their pale red-bricked facade, pierced by windows protected with forged-iron grills. The inside has all the austerity and calm of a cathedral, without the trimmings. The constantly cool temperatures that reign in the vast cellars full of barrels and hogsheads are surely one of the keys to what makes Vega-Sicilia so different from other wines. Refusing the

facility of marketing their wines as soon as possible and letting the customer cellar them until they are ready to drink, the owners only release their different wines after years of aging at the bodega Vega-Sicilia. This slow maturation takes place initially in wooden barrels of different sizes, then in bottles. The precise time and method of aging will depend on the wine, as there are three different products in the range. In every case, the idea is that a bottle

of Vega-Sicilia should be ready to drink when it reaches the customer. The youngest wine is called Valbuena and is sold when it is five years old. The vintage "Unico" is usually available ten years after its harvest. Finally there is a version of "Unico" that does not bear a vintage year, and which is a blend of wines from several harvests, some of them twenty years old.

Tasting

♦ *Valbuena 1991*
Nose of very ripe, almost cooked, fruit. Quite elegant, it gives a delicate impression, with lightly smoky overtones. The mouth is soft and round, and the finish fresher and more powerful than initially expected.

♦ *Vega-Sicilia 1985*
The nose is dark and dense, and at first is not very expressive. After a while, it opens up to spices, pepper, and a series of mint-like aromas. The mouth feel is soft and voluptuous, with a veritable bowl of berry fruit flavors that reveal themselves by stages. It has very fine texture, and its tannins are well-integrated. The flavors last well and finish clean and fresh. A complex, fascinating wine.

♦ *Vega-Sicilia 1994 (still in barrels)*
The nose is incredibly concentrated and powerful. New oak barrels have clearly been used, and there is a strongly mineral character, combined with black fruit and animal-type aromas. The mouth is just as concentrated as the nose. Everything is balanced by the delicious fruit flavors, and there are hints of resin and mint, which add a tang to the finish. Although the wine is still very young and is far from the end of its maturation, its texture is very fine. An extraordinary mixture of softness and freshness.

Taylor's Port

Since its foundation over three centuries ago the history of the house of Taylor's has typified the history of the fortified wine called port. The history of port as an exported wine began with merchants from the British Isles who came to Portugal to trade and barter local produce for cloth and other goods. Wine gradually became the center of their activity, and they decided to make it themselves. The current emblem of Taylor's is a double X, with the figure 4 above it. This was originally a brand-mark, literally branded onto bales of wool or cloth, and it dates back to this period. During the seventeenth and eighteenth centuries, the port market in England grew very rapidly. Repeated wars between France and England had slowed down imports of French produce, including wine, as the difficulties of wartime trade were compounded by increased customs duties or even total boycotts. Nature abhors a vacuum, and, among other sources, the wines of Portugal, considered to be sufficiently robust to stand the long sea journey, were a welcome replacement for those from Bordeaux.

This long sea crossing, however, posed a problem for some of the wines, in particular those of lower natural strength. It was found that a slight addition of grape spirit increased their strength sufficiently to enable them to resist the journey and its accompanying temperature changes. At one point, someone added the spirit a little earlier than usual, and the wine on arrival was found to be agreeably sweet and full of fruit flavors. Port, as we know it, was born. One of these early merchants was a young man from Yorkshire named Job Beardsley. He set up business in

Portugal in 1692, founding the company that was to become Taylor's Fladgate and Yeatman, otherwise known as Taylor's. Throughout its various partnerships and inheritances, it has remained a totally family-owned business.

What has characterized this house over the years is a permanent quest for excellence. Today, for example, Taylor's ports are kept for twice the average length of time in their cellars before shipping to markets, and the share of the top quality vintage ports in their production is far greater than elsewhere. The prices are accordingly higher, but this is not just the case for the younger wines, as Taylor's older vintage ports regularly fetch the highest prices at auctions. In all probability, the earliest bottlings of vintage port date from 1775, around ten years before the first bottlings of the top Bordeaux châteaux like Lafite. If there were to be a classification of the top "growths" of port, there is no doubt that Taylor's would be a first growth.

Such a ranking is not obtained overnight. In the case of port wines, and particularly with vintage ports, the span of aging required for wines to be at their best is reckoned in decades rather than in years. Such plain figures give no idea of the daring and perseverance that was required in a country where the vineyards were separated from the cellars and place of shipping by a range of steep mountains and fourty five miles or more. The only way of reaching the vineyards was on mule-back along some treacherous hillside tracks, until such time as the railways appeared in the late nineteenth century. The wines found their way down the Douro

Opposite: Taylor's Quinta do Vargellas estate runs down to the banks of the Douro, in its upper valley.
Above: Taylor's brand mark stands guard over its wines. Its origin harks back to those cloth merchants who came from Britain in the seventeenth century.

River on flat-bottomed boats that easily overturned. These had the predestined names of "barco rebello," which gives an idea of how hard they were to handle!

In 1727, Job Beardsley's son became the first British merchant to venture into what is known as the "upper country" to find the best quality wines that were—and still are—produced from grapes grown on these spectacularly arid and steep slopes of the upper Douro Valley. In 1774, he innovated again by purchasing a property in the Douro Valley, which continues to make wine for Taylor's today. In 1893, right in the middle of the phylloxera crisis, Taylor's went a step further by purchasing a farm, or "quinta," in the wildest part of the upper Douro. Quinta do Vargellas had been supplying Taylor's with wine since 1820, and a good proportion of their vintage wines still come from this estate today. The Portuguese word "quinta" signifies first and foremost a farm, but in the context of the wine-producing estates along the Douro Valley, one can compare the use of the term with that employed in Bordeaux for the word "château." Quinta do Vargellas is both farm, wine estate, family house, and reception center for Taylor's customers from around the

Above: Eiffel built this bridge that spans the Douro, linking Villa Nova de Gaia to Oporto. Left: The dining room at Taylor's, in Villa Nova de Gaia, epitomizes the tradition of English merchants who set up business here from the seventeenth century onwards.

world. It must also be one of the very few wine estates in the world to have its own railway station! Right by the house, the vegetable garden provides all the necessary fruit and vegetables, while the Vargellas pigs are the pride and joy of the owners. The low and beautiful house is whitewashed, like the walls that lead along the driveway. Its comfortable interior is deliciously cool in contrast to the arid heat that reigns outside on the stone terraces in the summer.

An excellent way of gaining an understanding of the way port's vineyards have been classified is to get up early and walk up the hill behind Vargellas. As the rising sun strikes the steeply terraced vineyards, one can see how some parts of the hills receive the sun's rays much earlier then others. Down by the river, the reflected light and warmer nighttime temperature will help the grapes to earlier maturity. Another important factor is the mineral nature of the soil, particularly

evident in the early spring, when the first tender green vine-shoots form a striking contrast with the blue-tinged ocher hues of the rock. Apart from the olive, and a few fruit trees huddled around the natural springs, wood is very scarce in this landscape. Even the vineyard posts used for trellising are made of slate! On these terraces that hug the hillside, forming contour patterns all over the landscape, the vines are often over seventy years old. Throughout the Douro Valley, most older vineyards contain a wide range of grape varieties, co-planted in each plot. Frank Yeatman, a partner of Taylor's in the early part of this century, innovated in the 1920's by planting a single variety per plot, thereby making it easier to determine the qualities of these varieties through the wines they produced.

Nowadays, planting is still carried out on terraces for the steeper slopes, but the walls require constant maintenance, as the winter rains take a heavy toll. As this work cannot be mechanized, its cost is difficult to sustain, and many vineyards now organize their plantings without the walls. Modern and traditional techniques also coexist in the winery at Taylor's, where stainless steel tanks are side by

side with granite-walled treading vats, called "lagares," in which foot treading of the grapes is still carried out. Men and women stomp for hours to the tune of local music, which helps keep spirits up while maintaining the necessary rhythm. This apparently primitive way of crushing the grapes is perpetuated not for the sake of local folklore, but because no better method has been found to obtain a maximum of color from the skins in a short space of time. This is vital in the case of port, as rapid extraction is imposed by other technical requirements. Both color and tannins are as present in vintage port as in the great dry red wines of the world, although the time that skins, which bear such ingredients, spend in contact with their juice is very much shorter.

TASTING

A short tasting was held in glorious, if unorthodox, surroundings. This wine was tasted outdoors, on the patio at Vargellas overlooking the Douro Valley, with a magnificent wysteria in full flower just a yard away. Not easy to concentrate with such surroundings, but what a delight. Imagination was not required to find floral aromas!

◆ *Taylor's 1970*
Very deep color and an extremely concentrated nose, with layers of different fruit aromas, followed by jams, spices, roasted coffee, and tobacco leaves. The mouth manages to seem both smooth and firm. Delicate fruit just about wraps itself around a fairly austere body. A very elegant wine, perfectly balanced, that may be drunk or kept for another ten years or so. This could be the ideal port to drink at the turn of the coming millennium, as it combines the wealth of the past with pleasure of the moment and hope for the future.

Quinta do Noval

The Douro Valley is one of the most spectacular vineyard sites in the world. This exceptional geographic situation has been complemented by exceptional legislation regarding the wine produced there. Few are aware that this was one of the earliest wine-producing areas to precisely define the zones where vineyards would be authorized, with a clear objective of controlling both quantity and quality. This took place in the early eighteenth century, but wines from Portugal had been widely exported since the fourteenth century, thanks to the seafaring capacity of the Portuguese. The word "Port" started to be used around 1675 to describe the wines that were shipped from the town of Oporto, on the mouth of the Douro River. In 1756, roughly 150 years before a similar movement began in France, the Marquis of Pombal, who was prime minister to the king of Portugal Joseph I, laid down a charter which prepared the way for one of the first regulated appellations in the world. This reform set out to maintain high quality standards in the wines produced by precisely indicating vineyard placement and surface area. The production area is about sixty five miles inland from the town of Oporto. The landscape is particularly hilly in this part of Portugal, which influences the nature of the wines. These variations have been taken into account by the regulations that govern today's production. Each vineyard plot is classified by a letter, following a scale which runs from "A," for the best sites, to "E." Many parameters come to bear in this classification: altitude, degree of slope, orientation, soil type, yield, and others. No other

Opposite: The landscape is molded by terraces that allow the vines to cling to the slopes.
Above: A long alley covered with vines leads up to the Quinta.

system in the world is as comprehensive and rigorous in the definition of what constitutes quality in terms of soil and meso-climate. The best vineyards are not those nearest to the coast. These are to be found close to the Douro River or its various tributaries, some far inland where rainfall is much scarcer. The mountains that separate the Port vineyards from the town which gives them its name take most of the rain coming from the Atlantic Ocean. The remainder falls on the western vineyards, while the upper Douro Valley is very dry. During its passage to the ocean from its sources in Spain, the Douro has carved and eroded the rock, leaving steep slopes which man, over the centuries, has patiently organized into terraces in order to cultivate crops. It is a considerable achievement to have planted vines and olive trees on these narrow and fragile strips that cling to the mountainside, and a tribute to man's perseverance in the face of such adverse conditions. The first glimpse of the Douro Valley is an exceptionally intense experience. The view is spectacular, and the narrow, twisty road constantly reminds one that there are precipitous drops at every bend. Just before reaching Quinta do Noval, things become slightly calmer, enabling one to admire the work of the vine-growers who have sculpted the landscape in such an extraordinary way. A long stone cobbled path, transformed into a sheltered alleyway by trellised vines that grow over, leads up to the farmhouse where, under a huge cedar tree, the heady perfumes of orange and lemon blossoms are waiting to reward the traveler. Noval's vineyards are in the Pinhao Valley, which runs into the upper reaches of the Douro. Its production has a particular place among the best port producers. Although its vineyard holding is not the largest, it is of top quality, consisting of 218 acres all classed in the "A" category. Founded just a century ago, Noval has constantly innovated in a world where tradition tends to dominate. In the 1920's, and then again in the 1950's, this house created new types of port wines. More recently

Left: Huddled against the mountain, the attractive whitewashed buildings of Quinta do Noval. "Quinta" is the Portuguese word for farm.
Below: Wood is of great importance in the aging of port. These barrels, known as "pipes," are waiting to be rinsed, prior to being filled with wine.

it became the first Port house to insist on maturing and bottling all its wines on the property in the Douro—rather like a Bordeaux château. Noval's best wines come from the Quinta's own vineyards.

There are two distinct types of port wine in the top category. Both originate from a single vintage year, and their principal difference stems from their respective aging processes. "Colheita" means "harvest" in Portuguese, and the word is used to describe wines that spend many years in large wood barrels before bottling. The English word "vintage" is used for wines that are bottled two years after harvest and which therefore age in the bottle for upwards of twenty years in customers' cellars. Colheitas age in barrels at the producer's cellars. Quinta do Noval produces both types of port, but they are particularly renowned as the producers of that rarest and most expensive of vintage ports, the mythical Nacional.

A single bottle of Quinta do Noval Nacional 1931 was sold for the sum of 5,900 dollars in 1988. This wine, like all vintage ports, is only made in those years when its quality is deemed to be worthy of its reputation, and its annual production rarely exceeds three thousand bottles. What makes it so special is the fact that the plants that produce it are not grafted, like those which existed in Europe before phylloxera destroyed the original vineyards at the end of the nineteenth century. Nobody seems to know why three small plots around the house are not affected by the dreaded louse that causes all other vines to be grafted onto resistant American root-stock. The grape varieties authorized to make Port wines are numerous, but only a few are generally considered to be capable of producing the highest quality. These are called Touriga Nacional, Touriga Francesca, Tinta Rouriz, Tinta Barroca, and Tinta Cão. The word "nacional" does not derive from the first of these varieties, but from the fact that its vines conserve a direct link with the soil of the mother-country, unfiltered by any foreign root-stock. When those in charge of great wines talk

of their production, their modesty is often striking, and Christian Seely, the managing director of Noval, is a perfect example. In his opinion, Noval's Nacional hardly requires any intervention on the part of its makers! In the case of a great wine, there is nothing that man could do to compensate for any deficiency in the quality of the raw material. The most sophisticated technology in the world can help to make the most of grapes, but it can never provide the extra dimension

that makes one wine seem truly great, and another merely good. Christian Seely defines this dimension around two measures: the intensity and the duration of the sensations received when tasting a wine. When taken this far, the apparently mysterious, but eminently subjective, notion of perfection brings us into the realm of aesthetics.

TASTING

A tasting of fourteen vintages of such a mythical wine can only leave one with an emotionally charged memory of an exceptional occasion. Here are a couple of the more memorable moments.

♦ *Nacional 1991*
The latest vintage available at the time of tasting, as the 1994 had not yet been "declared." Very deep color, and great intensity and complexity on the nose. Successive whiffs of chocolate, herbs, spices, and something like mint rush to the nose, followed by a layer of smoked aromas that remind one of charcuterie. All this seems extremely fresh. Although very young, the wine is tightly knit, both austere and elegant through its sweetness. The flavors linger on for minutes on the palate.

♦ *Nacional 1963*
Although almost thirty years older than the 1991, this wine seems, incredibly, more concentrated. Having once tasted it previously during a memorable meal in Paris, I was aware of its potential. The color is dark as ink, and to give the nose the space to show its paces, it should be opened the previous day. An hour after opening, it managed to reveal concentrated layers of densely ripe fruit, mingled with spices, whose flavors filled the mouth. Certainly one of the most extraordinary wines that I have ever had the good fortune to taste. Still young at over thirty-two years, it appeared a third of its age.

Johann Joseph Prüm

All around the small, picturesque town of Bernkastel, the Mosel River radiates a feeling of tranquillity that comes from its gentle pace, revealed by its broad loops. The valley is narrow, and, on whichever side faces the sun, vines climb almost from the river's edge to 650 feet above the water level, up impressively steep slopes. Opposite the township of Wehlen, the vineyard called Sonnenuhr is the perfect illustration of such topography. Right in its center, a rocky outcrop acts as support for a sundial that enables Manfred Prüm to calculate how much sun is falling on his plot within the Sonnenuhr from his home across the river. If the ripening of the Riesling grape owes much to direct sunlight, helped along by the reverberation from the river's surface, its complex perfumes have to do with the shale-type soils whose permeability enables these vineyards to be planted vertically to the slope, almost without any terraces to hold back the soil.

This soil can soak up water like a sponge, and, like a sponge, it can also retain water in order to return it to the plant. This enables the grapes to ripen slowly, giving the wines of Mosel their extremely fine aromas. When he lived in Trier during Roman times, the poet Ausonius, who came from Bordeaux, sang the praises of these wines. For centuries, the Prüm family included legates of the archbishop of Trier, and then the extensive family vineyard was split up. It was Johann Joseph Prüm, whose name figures on the estate's labels, who raised the levels of its wines at the end of the nineteenth century. Today his grandson, Doctor Manfred Prüm, manages the estate. Tasting wines with him is a memorable experience that provides a unique opportunity to get closer to

Opposite: With the township of Wehlen lying across the Mosel River, the steep slopes of the Sonnenuhr vineyard, just downstream from Berkastel.
Above: A detail of a tiled panel in the Prüm residence.

understanding, in the most civilized way possible, the rich potentials of the Riesling grape. He serves his wines slowly, one by one, following the rhythm of the river that slowly flows by in front of the windows of his house. Time is taken to approach the wines gradually, letting them soften and go through their paces according to the various temperatures as they warm slightly in the glass. Manfred Prüm does not treat wine as something to be analyzed and resumed in a set of figures. Tasting wine is a vector of pleasure, a way of understanding the relationship between the taster and his wine, and requires introspection as well as verbal exchange. He recognizes, in all modesty, that his wines need more time than most to be approached, and indeed some of them appear to have the gift of eternal life, so youthful are they after fifteen or

twenty years. A Kabinett Bernkastler of 1979, for example, tasted in 1996, had the soft greenness of the river and the strongly mineral edge of the soil: its acidity had become rounded so as to seem almost spherical, and there was not a trace of any fatigue due to aging. Alcohol is never overpresent in such wines, as their alcohol content is usually only around eight percent. The wines of J.J. Prüm are best, according to Dr Prüm, when enjoyed at one of three stages in their long lives: with the fruit of their youth, in other words within the first two years after their bottling; when they reach their phase of harmony, which is after five to eight years, depending on the type of wine; and when they are fully mature, which is usually after at least thirty years. In the end, the only thing that really counts is to drink them whenever they give one

Opposite (far side): Built in the slate rock of the vineyards, the Prüm residence, on the edge of the Mosel River.
Opposite (near side): Sundial in the Sonnenuhr vineyard. One of these is shown on the J.J.Prüm estate wine labels.
Below: This map, dating from the fourteenth century, shows the town of Bernkastel surrounded by vineyards.

pleasure. For Manfred Prüm, a great wine possesses concentration, while giving the greatest of pleasure. What are the respective shares of nature and man in making a great wine? His answer is to quote a professor at the famous Enological School of Geisenheim, who said, "Being a good artisan is important, but having good grapes is even more important! " In other words, the character of a wine cannot be disguised by clever wine-making. In the case of these fine German wines, alcohol is naturally light, and it is not allowed to be reinforced by chaptalisation. Thus the true nature of the fruit comes through, unadulterated, to the glass, and with it the flavor that those grapes have derived from soil and climate conditions. Trying to go against this can only lead to failure, and the loss of the desired degree of finesse. Here lies the miracle of Germany's great wines: a strong personality with a surprisingly light alcoholic content.

Wine remains a living substance, evolving in a way that is not always predictable. Tastes for wine also change, through time as well as from one culture to another. The combination of these variables explains the changing popularities of particular wines, from one country to another, but some time spent exploring the subtleties of any wine will soon reveal its potential.

TASTING

◆ *Spätlese Wehlener Sonnenuhr 1981*
A touch of lightness is given by a small amount of carbonic gas that has been deliberately kept in the wine. This makes it seem almost airy, despite a small amount of residual sugar. The aromas are very much floral, with hints of citrus fruit and linden. The acidity is strong at first then progressively blends itself into the body of the wine. With just seven or eight degrees of alcohol, the wine seems incredibly young and powerful. An ideal wine for contemplating the sky!

◆ *Beerenauslese Wehlener Sonnenuhr 1976*
With its color of roasted peaches, this wine has a suave, almost buttery nose, wrapped in layers of walnut, hazelnut, and exotic fruit. These aromas slowly build up in the mouth, with elegance and power, to reach an explosion of flavors. The finish is magnificent, pure and fresh, with the flavors lingering. Successful in every department and absolutely delicious.

Maximin Grünhaus

Under the Roman Empire, Trier was the most important town of northern Europe. Founded by the Emperor Augustus in the year 15 B.C., it progressively became a military, administrative, and university center. Taking its name from the Mosel River and its two main tributaries, the Saar and the Ruwer, this fine wine-growing area, spread out along the banks that face the sun, is remarkably homogenous. The Saar runs into the Mosel upstream of Trier, and the Ruwer joins it just downstream. The Maximin Grünhaus estate is so well-known and long established that its name is allowed to appear alone on the labels of its bottles, without any town being mentioned. This is a privilege shared by a small number of estates in Germany, such as Schloss Johannisberg, and is reminiscent of the Burgundian Grand Cru system. The site has been occupied at least since Roman times, as is shown by pottery remains found here. In all probability, a Roman country villa was built exactly where the current house stands. A little later, in the ninth century, the Holy Roman Emperor Otto I, who succeeded Charlemagne, gave the land to the Benedictine monastic order. They founded the abbey of Saint Maximin, and the cellars of the estate date from this period.

A great Riesling can only come from an exceptional vineyard site, combining a perfect meso-climate with the right type of soil. The slightest variation in growing or making techniques will have a considerable influence on the wine, but none more than the specific vineyard situation. The monks who cultivated these spectacular hillside vineyards for centuries grew to understand all the nuances that the land could communicate to the

Above: Nobody knows why the manor house is called Grünhaus, or "the green house." It may have been painted green when it was first built, or the name may refer to the densely vegetated surroundings. **Opposite:** The building known as " Mary's house " is Carl von Schubert's residence.

finished wine. Although the vineyard of Maximin Grünhaus is a single hillside slope, it is divided into three distinct parts: Bruderberg, Herrenberg, and Abtsberg. The wines from the Bruderberg were destined for the consumption of the lay brothers, those from the Herrenberg for the senior fathers, whereas the Abtsberg, which produced the very best wines, was reserved for the Abbot and his guests. In fact, the monks went even further, distinguishing two different plots within the Abtsberg.

Surrounded by a forest which acts as a windbreak, and sheltered up in a tiny valley that keeps it away from the flood-prone Ruwer River, this vineyard overlooks a fine manor house that has belonged to the von Schubert family since 1882. Dr. Carl von Schubert scrupulously respects nature by only using organic processes in his vineyard: manure comes from his own cows, and no chemical fungicides are used. He has fixed himself the clear goal of preserving this exceptional vineyard site in all its natural rich-

Above: The Herrenberg vineyard with its crooked gateway.

temperature at soil level can reach 60°C (140°F) in midsummer, but this doesn't seem to prevent the wines having incomparable finesse. A large proportion of the wines are vinified as dry, or "trocken," but whatever their degree of residual sugar, all taste incredibly pure and fresh. Although Carl von Schubert is in favor of intervening as little as possible in the vineyard, there is no sign of a "laissez-faire" approach in the wine-making, and the mastery is apparent in the clear-cut flavors. When weather conditions are right, more than twenty different wines are made at Maximin Grünhaus, which necessitates a very precise control and guidance of each and every one. The overall wine-making philosophy is to make wines that are a pleasure to drink, whatever their respective type or level may be. The top wines, usually destined for long cellar-ing, come from late harvests which require up to six different pickings in the steep slopes of the Abtsberg in order to select only those bunches that have been concentrated by botrytis. Wherein lies the sign of greatness in a wine? Dr. von Schubert considers that a great wine, under the right circumstances, is capable of generating a form of vibration in the human spirit that can give one access to something otherwise inaccessible. The very idea that these wines are directly descended from those that were made for centuries by monks can only increase this form of expectancy.

TASTING

What is remarkable in these wines is the immediate pleasure they give, while showing clearly that they will be around for a long time. Those who know them best say that they can go through a poor phase for a few years, during their aging process.

◆ *Abtsberg Kabinett trocken 1995*
A sharp, mineral-like edge. The mouth feel is very fresh, and the acidity develops gradually without shocking the palate. The

final flavors are gently mineral and smoky, like many fine Rieslings.

◆ *Abtsberg Trockenbeerenauslese 1995*
The nose is full of a delicious series of honeyed aromas, pushed along by flowers and fruit. The most striking impression in the mouth is the silky-smooth texture, both round and lively. The flavors last a full minute on the palate.

ness, as it was a thousand years ago. Such wisdom and moderation have a price: the yields are just half of those generally obtained in the area. On a shale soil which warms up rapidly, and with a perfect angle to the sun's rays, the vineyard is able to concentrate the natural grape flavors. In some parts of the vineyard, the

Schloss Johannisberg

There are few actives vineyard in the world that can be said to have played a key part in the history of wine. In the Rheingau, Schloss Johannisberg, overlooking the Rhine Valley, can claim such a role, just as Clos de Vougeot in Burgundy. From the fourth and fifth centuries onwards, the arrival of Christianity and the breakup of the Roman Empire implied that Europe's center gradually shifted northward from Rome. A few centuries later, Charlemagne established his capital in Aix-la-Chapelle, and the Rhine River became the symbolic center of Europe. Legend has it that the emperor, looking across from his palace of Jugelheim, noticed that snow melted sooner on the slopes of the Johannisberg hill than on the surrounding countryside and therefore ordained that vines be planted there. Vines certainly were planted around this time, as we have written proof of the presence of vineyards at Johannisberg just three years after Charlemagne's death, in 817. The fifteenth parallel runs right through the vineyard, immediately in front of today's castle, which is a clear indication that this is near Europe's northern limit for the ripening of grapes. Within such latitudes, perfect exposure to the sun's rays is of capital importance to the production of fine wine. The undulating slopes that run between the Rhine and the Taunus mountains face mainly south. No doubt the monastic wine growers were aware of this advantage, as from the thirteenth century onwards, the Rheingau became one vast vineyard. What certainly helped this development was the capacity of the Rhine to safely carry any quantity of heavy goods, such as wine, in barrels.

It is fairly logical to assume that today's quality German white wines resemble those of former times. The combination of a cool

Above: The entrance to the cellars of Schloss Johannisberg.

Above: Stone marker for the fifteenth parallel, which runs through the vineyard. Opposite (upper): One of the large casks dedicated to the Metternich family on the occasion of the 150th anniversary of their ownership. Opposite (lower): The vaulted cellars of the château.

climate and an absence of chaptalisation result in wines of low alcoholic strength, and as these wines have only between seven and ten percent alcohol, balance has to be acheived by the quality of the Riesling grape's acidity and other ingredients. The origins of this grape are uncertain, but it seems to have been planted in Germany since at least the sixteenth century. In such a climate, this grape variety has many advantages, among which is its capacity to ripen late in the year, thereby allowing a build-up of sugars without a drop in acidity due to the heat of the sun. Riesling is the sole grape planted on the seventy nine acres of Schloss Johannisberg, and it is known to

temporal powers. The Benedictine monks administered the estate for almost a thousand years, until both land and monastery were purchased in 1716 by the abbey-prince Fulda, who built the existing château. Secularized in 1802, the estate became the property of the Prince of Orange. Napoleon captured it in 1806 and gave it to Kellerman, one of his generals. Then, by one of history's ironic twists, it was given to his arch enemy Metternich by the Congress of Vienna, for services rendered to the cause of peace. The Metternich family still owns it today.

Under the château, the cellars house a marvelous treasure of old vintages that date back to 1748. The estate buildings grouped around the château harbor an ultra-modern winery and a restaurant, which has a splendid view of the vineyard and the Rhine. The vineyards surround the château and its park, and walking around them is the best way of getting to know this exceptional place dedicated not only to wine culture, but also to music.

TASTING

♦ *Spätlese trocken 1993*
The nose is steely and bright, quite austere with a smoky edge to it. Mineral aromas reminiscent of the slatelike soil come through gradually. The crispness sets the mouth tingling, and one is surprised by such a firm grip behind such apparent lightness.

♦ *Eiswein 1993*
This is a wine of great contrasts. The nose gives off a concentration of honey and citrus and other fruit. The acidity gives a cutting edge to these smells. It comes through so powerfully in the mouth that one hesitates between pleasure and discomfort. Fruit flavors are incredibly concentrated and gradually calm down to a slow and delicious declension of the most delicate of aromas.

have been here since the seventeenth century. This estate was the first to make a whole range of wines from Riesling, ranging from the perfectly dry to the very fine and rare sweet wines. A spätlese from Schloss Johannisberg was the first German wine to be made with grapes affected by what is known as "noble rot." Spätlese means "late harvest," and there are at least four wine-producing regions, all famous for wines made from late-harvested grapes that have been more or less affected by noble rot, that claim to have been the first to use the process. Tokay from Hungary, Ruster Ausbruch from Austria, Sauternes from France, or sweet wines from the Rhine Valley in Germany all have claims

to fame, not to mention the Cotnari from Roumania. It seems fairly clear that the "azsu" process used in Tokay or in Rust is the ancestor of this type of wine, and that sweet wines were made at Johannisberg somewhat earlier than at Château Yquem, in Sauternes.

Schloss Johannisberg is an imposing château dating from the seventeenth century, with a much older church nearby, although both have undergone extensive repairs since the war. Perched on the crest of the Johannisberg hill, it is visible for miles around. Its history is intimately mingled with that of this part of Germany, where politics and religion have constantly made, and then unmade,

Weingut Robert Weil

Towards the end of the nineteenth century, Germany's greatest wines from the Rhine and Mosel valleys sold for higher prices than the best of Bordeaux. Wilhelm Weil, the great-grandson of Robert Weil, the founder of this family estate, has a small collection of old vintages, including one from 1893. This wine sold in London in the early years of this century for exactly three times the price of a bottle of Château Latour. If one day, the top German wines recover the place that they formerly held on the price scale of world wines, then it will largely be due to the quality of wines like those of Weingut Robert Weil.

Slightly set back from the Rhine, the village of Kiedrich is sheltered from the main flow of the tourist hordes that come to the Rheingau from neighboring big cities like Frankfurt, Cologne, and Mainz. Looking at the perfectly restored dwellings, it is hard to imagine that this village used to be poor. Opposite the bell tower of the gothic church of St. Valentine, the oldest of the region, lies the southwest facing vineyard called Gräfenberg, which means the count's hill. In former times this vineyard was reserved for the town's leading citizens who had access to the best exposed vines, and thus to the best wine. When Robert Weil purchased a plot of the Gräfenberg, it was the start of his activities as a wine-maker. Previously, he taught German at Paris' Sorbonne University, but was forced to leave when the Franco-Prussian War broke out in 1870. The estate now comprises about 125 acres and an ultramodern winery. Its range of wines is justly considered as being part of the very best of contemporary German production.

Wilhelm Weil is a firm believer in the quality of a wine being obtained, above all, in the vineyard. Harvesting is carried out by hand, and the yields are deliberately low for the region. This—and

Above and opposite: The Gräfenberg vineyard, formerly reserved for the town's leading citizens.
Opposite: A dining room in the estate house.

an excellent vineyard—probably explains why Weil is the only Rheingau producer to have been able to make the full range of wines, from Trocken to Trockenbeerenauslese, every year for the past eight. In the winery, fermentation is carried out as slowly as possible in order to maintain the finest and most delicate aromas. For the same reasons, the traditional wooden barrels have been abandoned, and, after fermenting in stainless steel tanks, the wines are aged in bottles. The wines of Weingut Robert Weil have brilliance and give instant pleasure. Wilhelm Weil's wide-ranging curiosity and sense of perfection push him to experiment constantly, which ensures that such high levels will be maintained.

Above: The house has been perfectly renovated in the local tradition and harbors offices and reception rooms.

◆ *Kiedricher Gräfenberg Riesling Trockenbeerenauslese 1995*
A very rich nose for such a young wine. It shows concentrated mass of crystalized and citrus fruit, followed by raisins, coffee, chocolate, and caramel. In the mouth, this richness is transcended by a fine acidity that enables the aromas to continue for minutes. This beautiful wine will surely last a hundred years!

TASTING

◆ *Kiedricher Gräfenberg Riesling Spätlese Trocken 1995*
The nose is fascinating, with its smoky and mineral accents. The first sensation in the mouth is of something as round and polished as à marble. Then the fruit comes through, very crisp and long, and finishes on a pleasant touch of bitterness that gives additional body. Balance is achieved by a remarkable combination of power and delicacy.

Tokay

One of the world's most mythical wines, that great sweet wine called Tokay, takes its name from a small town in the north-west corner of Hungary, close to the borders of Slovakia and the Ukraine. Its history is so rich and so unusual that it is closer than any other wine to symbolizing the spirit and aspiration of a nation. What other wine appears in the words of the national anthem? Whereas Louis XIV of France described Tokay as "a wine for kings, the king of wines," the Tsars of Russia used to dispatch a regiment of cossacks every year to Tokay to ensure that their annual consignment of the precious nectar arrived safe and sound in Moscow or Saint Petersburg. During the seventeenth and eighteenth centuries, Tokay's reputation was at a peak, and not only was it served at the tables of all the crowned heads of Europe, but it was also shipped to the cellars of wine connoisseurs in New World countries. There is no doubt that the ruling dynasty of the then Austro-Hungarian Empire, the Hapsburgs, helped to start off this craze through their belief in the medicinal qualities of Tokay. They believed in particular that the rarest of Tokay wines, the royal Eszencia, had almost magical properties, and would either prolong life or, at the very least, ease the passage into life hereafter. The extreme concentration of Eszencia meant that it was administered by the spoonful to the dying, possibly as a sample of paradise. Such beliefs have left their mark in contemporary Hungary, as the sweet Aszu is considered to be beneficial for health to the point where one can

Opposite: Disnoko's vineyard, at the entrance to the Tokay area, coming from Budapest. Old and new ways of planting coexist in the vineyards, as can be seen from the varying densities.
Above: The pediment of Hetzolo, which used to belong to the Rakoczi family.

still find it in dispensaries. Tokay Aszu has become a national symbol, both for curing ailments and for the proper celebration of great events.

Placed right in the center of Europe, Hungary has lived throughout the centuries under the rule of various powers from different horizons. Romans, Huns, Ottomans, Austrians, and, more recently, Russians have each spent more time running the country than the Magyars themselves. But in this ancient kingdom of Hungary that goes back to the year 1000, national pride has never resigned in the face of occupation, and it has often been in the area of Tokay that resistance has been at its fiercest. At the southern tip of the vineyard, the town of Tokay is cooled by a river which used to carry goods far and beyond. In order to identify them, wines from the surrounding hills took on the name of the river port at which they were put on

Above: The atmosphere in the tasting cellars of Tokay are a reminder that Transylvania is not far away!
Below: The castle of Sarospatak, one of many that belonged to the Rakoczi princes.
Opposite: In the labyrinths of Tokay's underground cellars ages one of the most mysterious of the world's great wines.

board ship, exactly as was the case for the town of Bordeaux in France.

On these volcanic hillsides, the Romans made wine from the third century onwards, but nothing much is known about these wines. It was only in the seventeenth century that precise written descriptions existed of the way in which wine from the Tokay area was made with "Aszu" or botrytised grapes that increased the sugar content. This would make Tokay the oldest appellation in the world, as shortly afterwards the vineyard limits within which this particular wine could be made were laid down. As to their reputation, the wines from Tokay benefited from political events in the same way as those from the Douro Valley. In 1703, Ferenc Rakoczi, a Protestant Prince of Transylvania, an autonomous province three times the actual size of Hungary, took up arms against the Catholic ruler of Austria and lost the battle. By one of history's mysterious turns, he ended up in France at the court of Louis XIV, also Catholic, but apparently not entirely neutral in this matter. Out of gratitude, Rakoczi gave the French king some bottles of Tokay Aszu. These went down very well indeed, and the word got out.

Under forty years of communist rule, much of the vineyard was nationalized, and wine-making became controlled by a state monopoly that took the name of "kombinat." This organized production in the area to supply large quantities of dry or semi-sweet white wine for the Russian market, neglecting the great sweet wines. The underground cellars, which had long since transformed the subsoil around the towns and villages into something like a rabbit warren, remained intact. These figure among the treasures of Tokay. Originally dug as shelter against Turkish invasions, some of them go back to the thirteenth century. Cellars like those in the townships of Sarospatak, Tokay, Mad, or Tolsva store the wine for years under perfect conditions. Naturally dark, cool, and damp, like those in Champagne, they allow Tokay wine to age slowly. As to the vineyard owners, only the smallholders escaped having their land confiscated. They were, however, obliged to sell their grapes to the state monopoly, merely keeping back enough to make wine for their own consumption. Equipment was difficult to find, and almost impossible to buy, so the tiny vineyard plots were worked by hand. This system still survives, several years after the fall of the communist regime, as 15,000 different owners share the 6,000 hectares that make up Tokay today, which means the average plot is around one acre.

Since 1990, the Hungarian state has been gradually returning the vineyards that it still owns to private ownership. Families that had lost their lands have managed to get some back, and smallholders have enlarged their plots. There are now

fifteen owners or companies whose vineyard estates cover between 125 and 250 acres, and among these are a dozen in which foreign investors have teamed up with Hungarians in joint ventures. This double movement, with a large number of small vine-growers increasing their holdings to become viable, and large companies bringing in equipment and skills, looks like being Tokay's chance for its Azsu wines to return to their former glory. In the midst of estates that are re-emerging, the odd company building sprouts the name "château" or "bodega," but this can hardly be qualified as a major colonizing operation, rather a genuine will to attract attention to these truly great wines. The nationality of the investors can be guessed, in most cases, from the company names, whether they be French, Spanish, or British. Châteaux Disnoko, Pajzos, Hetzolo, Megyer, Messzelato Dulo, Bodegas Oremus, or Royal Tokaji Wine

Above: Great wines require considerable investments, like those made at Disnoko. Opposite: The modern winery at Disnoko, designed by a Hungarian architect. Below: Eszencia slowly fermenting in glass demi-johns. The natural sugar levels are so high that it will barely reach five percent alcohol.

Company each have specific structures and their own vision of Tokay wines. In one of the oldest vineyards in Europe, they share the paradoxical experience of being, in many respects, pioneers who are reinventing or rediscovering wine-making

traditions with some help from modern means.

Tokay's wines were exported and gained renown throughout the Europe of the seventeenth century by merchants from Poland, France, Scotland, and Germany. Today, a mere eight percent of the vineyard has been conceded to companies with foreign investors, but the impact of their investment will be far greater than this apparently small share. Grouped together in an association called "Tokay Renaissance," their declared aim is to help Tokay regain its former glory. The different approaches of all the new owners will gradually allow the development of individual styles within this region where, for too long, wine-making had been standardized under the state company. Great wine is necessarily rare, and Tokay Aszu is no exception, with its handpicked grapes affected by botrytis. Not all years provide the required conditions to produce Aszu grapes. The high esteem and value of such vineyards is summed up by an old Hungarian saying: "It is not given to everybody to own vines in Tokay."

TASTING

◆ *Royal Tokaji Wine Company Betsek Aszu 5 puttonyos 1991*
The nose smells of flowers and dried fruit with a slightly smoky overtone. Powerfully fresh in the mouth, with flavors of citrus fruit, and especially orange peel. It is as if the acidity were surfing on a sugar wave, giving an impression of elegance like an ice-skater. Very long finish.

◆ *Château Pajzos Aszu 4 puttonyos 1991*
The nose is soft and full of subtlety. Honey and beeswax are the main aromas. This gives a rounded feel to the mouth, and the acidity comes on progressively, carrying apricot and peach flavors. Right at the end there is a touch of bitterness, like fresh almonds, which gives added complexity.

◆ *Château Megyer Aszu 5 puttonyos 1993*
The nose covers a wide range of aromas: flowers, citrus fruit and resin, with a hint of smoke to finish. A mouthful of honey with freshness to lighten the feel, bring on delicious peach, apricot, and marmelade flavors. The balance between sugar and acidity promises harmonious aging. The wine appears more delicate than powerful for the moment, which makes it easier to enjoy.

◆ *Château Disnoko Aszu 6 puttonyos 1993*
Concentrated and complex on the nose, with fruit, honey, and hazelnut aromas. This is firm and fresh in the mouth, with a delicate feel to it and excellent balance lifted by a slight touch of bitterness at the end.

◆ *Bodegas Oremus Aszu 6 puttonyos 1972*
The smell seems dense but soft. The flavors include caramel, figs, prunes, tobacco, and coffee. Although the length is average, the balance is superb.

Rüster Ausbruch

This eastern extremity of Austria is situated right at the geographical heart of Europe and has, through the centuries, constantly been influenced alternatively by east and west. A brief look at its history illustrates this perfectly. When the Turks were stopped in their invasion of Europe at Vienna, they occupied the town of Rust, on the edge of the lake Neusiedl. After a long period under Austrian rule, the Austro-Hungarian Empire broke up, and Rust became part of Hungary, until 1921. Between the two world wars it was returned to Austria, only to fall back under Russian, and then Russian-influenced Hungarian control, in 1945. In 1956, it rejoined the free world by becoming part of Austria once again.

For five centuries, regimes changed faster then wine-making traditions at Rust, as its sweet wines have survived in a style that is probably close to those that were so fashionable in the fifteenth and sixteenth centuries. The natural qualities of its climate, together with the determination of those who have cultivated the vines there over the centuries, have brought about the survival and the development of a very ancient wine-making tradition. The Wenzel family came to Rust in the seventeenth century and started making wines that had already been made in Rust for several centuries. This is certified by the earliest export documents available, which date back to 1476. A few years later, in 1524, Queen Mary of Hungary granted the wine-makers of Rust the right to stamp a brand on their barrels, thus authenticating their production. In terms of wine, this is one of the earliest traces of branding, as well as being perhaps the first movement towards what was to become, much later, the idea of appellations linked to site. This latter notion is made very clear in the letters patent that

Opposite: Winter flooding from melting snow in the vineyards near the lake Neusiedl.
Above: The private reserve of one of the Wenzels' customers.

recognize the privilege in these terms: "as official testimony of the origins of the wines from the vineyards of our town of Rust and not from other vineyards, places or estates." In 1681, the Austrian emperor, Leopold I, confirmed the citizens of Rust in their privileges by granting them the right to govern their town, giving them the status of free town. Every deal has its compensation, and the emperor, who obviously knew his wine, stipulated that, in exchange for this privilege, the citizens of Rust would have to deliver to him a certain quantity of their Ausbruch wine every year. It was this autonomy that enabled the good citizens of Rust to maintain and develop its prosperity, and the beauty of its houses, which mostly date from this period, are living proof of their success.

A specific climatic factor has enabled the production of the great sweet wines of this area. Grapes acquire the very highest levels of sugars when they reach full maturity and then are shriveled up, and thus concentrated, by the attack of a fungus called *botrytis cinerea*. This mushroom will only develop under certain weather conditions, such as cool mornings followed by warm days, within a humid atmosphere. Rust is on the edge of a vast lake, called the Neusiedl, whose depth never exceeds 6.5 feet. This constant humidity, combined with the hot continental temperatures in late summer, provide ideal conditions for botrytis in the vineyards near the lakeshore.

Ausbruch has an individual style among sweet white wines, through the way it is made. This is very similar to that other great sweet wine from central Europe, the Tokay Azsu from Hungary. It involves adding the highly concentrated juice from botrytised grapes to sweet wine. Such techniques applied to naturally concentrated grapes produce wines that can age for a very long time. Because of its rareness, Ausbruch is only available in seventeen ounce bottles, and the production is usually reserved by collectors throughout the world almost as soon as the harvest has been brought in.

Robert Wenzel will soon be retiring and will hand on the reins of the small family estate of twenty five acres to his son, Michel, who will thus become the eleventh generation of Wenzels to make wine at Rust. The charm and the modesty of this family makes a visit truly delightful. In the depths of winter, snow covers the vineyards and surrounds the

houses whose brightly-colored facades light up at the slightest ray of sunshine. Pushing open the heavy wooden door through which cartloads of grapes squeeze every harvesttime, one enters a cobbled courtyard. The cellar and winery huddle under the dwelling house, and one tastes at a kitchen table in a small room that doubles as an office. A few yards away, Ausbruch from the last harvest is still fermenting and will slowly continue to do so until at least the following spring. Time stands still as the Wenzels pour their wines or show you the secret reserve cellars where some of their most faithful customers are able to store their precious bottles of Ausbruch. In such cases, their bin is marked with a small brass plate, to identify the lucky owner who lets them age gracefully until the right moment.

Below (upper): The houses at Rust have vaulted archways leading to the inner courtyard.
Below (lower): The slightest ray of sun brings out the colors of the baroque facades.
Opposite: The Wenzel cellars, which are under the family house.

◆ *Rüster Ausbruch 1993 - Furmint*
Satz vineyard
The aromas are floral and mineral, more restrained and elegant than the previous wine, and are revealed by stages. Although the wine obviously has great concentration, it is very fine-textured. The freshness of the finale shows all the lift necessary for long cellaring, probably longer than the sauvignon. This wine is a thoroughbred that requires patience and a discerning master.

TASTING

Within the total production of the Wenzel family, only 1,320 gallons of sweet wines will be made in a given year. The range of these sweet wines follows the German scale, with, in increasing order of concentration, Auslese, Beerenauslese, Ausbruch, and Trockenbeerenauslese. Ausbruch can be made every other year on average.

◆ *Rüster Ausbruch 1993 - Sauvignon Blanc*
Baumgarten vineyard.
It has a rich and exuberant nose, with powerful, mineral-type aromas. It needs time to open up and will benefit from decanting. It is surprisingly lively on the palate, without a trace of heaviness in the peach, apricot, and cherry flavors. A wine that will be at its best in about a generation's time, but will last much longer.

Klein Constantia

Great wines can come and go, in the manner of civilizations. That great sweet white wine of South Africa, Constantia, almost disappeared on two occasions, only to rise from its ashes like the phoenix, thanks to determined men who refused to allow one of the wine world's glories to slip into oblivion. Today, the original estate is divided into two separate entities, Klein Constantia and Groot Constantia. The founder of Constantia was Simon van der Stel, governor of the Dutch Cape province at the end of the seventeenth century. He obtained from the Dutch East India Company an estate about the size of the city of Amsterdam, just behind Table Mountain, and a few miles inland from the ocean. He didn't choose the site on the spur of the moment. The valley's natural beauty and ideal climate would, in most cases, have been sufficient to make up the mind of an aspiring settler thinking of agricultural activities, but in the case of wine, Van der Stel required further proof that the soil was suitable for his project. He therefore systematically dug soil samples at various points of the planned estate and sent these for analysis. Only when he became convinced of the low fertility, granite-based nature of this soil did he make his decision, in 1685, to plant vineyards here, opposite False Bay. Once planted and production started, the

Opposite: Part of Klein Constantia's vineyard, overlooking False Bay.
Above: Freshly harvested white grapes come into the winery to be pressed.

wine's reputation came quickly. The first tasting notes from Holland came back in 1692 with the following message: "The wine of Constantia is greatly superior to everything we have received to date, and it is a pity that it is available in such small quantities."

According to historical investigations, it appears that the grape varieties used by Van der Stel and his successors were numerous and came from various European countries. What seems certain is that the famous Constantia wine was sweet, and that there was both a red and a white, the second being the rarest and most expensive. The varieties used included Muscat of Alexandria and Muscat of Frontignan. Both are still widely planted in South Africa under the names of "hannepoot" and "muskadel" respectively. The very sweet style of such a wine would have been in fashion at that time.

Above : The vineyard in the shadow of Table Mountain.
Below: The home of Lowell Jooste is in the pure "Cape Dutch" style of the first colonists.

Above: The Huguenot monument in Franschoek. Huguenots played an important role in developing the vineyard after the initial Dutch plantations.
Opposite: Tall vine plants of the Muscat of Frontignan variety.
Below: The fine vaulted cellars, built of whitewashed bricks.

Constantia went through troubled times, but even after the estate was split into two, each part tried successively to raise the standards of their wine to top levels. In the early part of the eighteenth century, constantia had the reputation of producing the best wine. Two Swedish botanists decided to find out what were the reasons behind this. Usually, when two experts give an opinion on the same subject, one can expect two totally different viewpoints. This occasion was no exception, as one expert firmly maintained that the soil's characteristics explained the wine's quality, whereas the other was sure that the key role was played by the climate. To give them their due, our two experts probably forgot that science, like wine, requires a little time to put such things in perspective. Observation of the interactions between soil, climate, and grape variety, in the case of wines that are destined to be kept for years before being drunk, probably requires at least a generation before conclusions can be drawn, but in fact they had isolated the two factors which, when combined, produce what is known as "terroir." Terroir is an essential ingredient of any great wine, although the human factor must be added to enable things to happen. This human factor was to show itself again in 1778, when Hendrick Cloete acquired Groot Constantia, which had been totally abandoned for a number of years. This man's courage and willpower, together with his search for excellence, were enough to regain this wine's reputation in a short space of time, even if some of his methods would not be applicable today. In order to protect his vines from predators, for instance, he stationed a hundred slaves in the vineyard with instructions to swat any insect that they saw on the grapes. Despite such "politically incorrect" techniques, he obtained the result of a wine whose reputation was attested to by many writers, from Klopstock to Jane Austen, and from Dickens to Baudelaire. The royal courts of Europe were so enamored with this wine that the price soared almost to the level of the world's most expensive wine of that time, Hungary's Tokay. Two deadly menaces then struck Constantia at the end of the nineteenth century: phylloxera and taxation, which between them removed this great sweet wine from cellars, and practically from memories, for almost one hundred years.

In 1980, Duggie Jooste bought the Klein Constantia estate and decided to awaken the sleeping beauty. After much effort and considerable investment, the magnificent vineyard that climbs the slopes of Mount Constantia has reemerged. Both vineyard and winery have been renovated, but Duggie Jooste was particularly interested in finding out exactly what had made the sweet wine of Constantia so great. Extensive searching turned up a few bottles of Constantia from the nineteenth century, which were duly tasted and analyzed, and experiments were carried out in the vineyard. These studies led to the planting of Muscat of Frontignan in the part of the vineyard where the soil is the least fertile and made of broken-down granite. Together with his son Lowell, who runs the estate, Jooste began his attempts to re-create the great sweet wine. The first vintages are encouraging, and now time must tell its tale, as the vines become mature and the wine ages in bottles. It must be remembered that patience is an intrinsic part of any great wine.

♦ *Constantia 1991*
A wonderful depth of roasted aromas come to the nose. Under this impression of sun-cooked fruit come notes of nuts, spices, and roses, which finish with a hint of toast and cocoa beans. The mouth feel is very full, but less powerful than one would expect from the smell. Everything is smoothly round, roasted, not over-sweet. The aftertaste is clear-cut and very pleasant.

Opposite (upper): Sunset in the garden at Klein Constantia.
Opposite (lower): The heart of Klein Constantia lies just inside this doorway.
Above: Handpicking of grapes at harvesttime, which is around April in the Southern Hemisphere.
Left: Late harvested grapes are picked when almost dried out to increase concentration of sugar and aromas.

KLEIN CONSTANTIA
ESTATE WINE
Vin de Constance
1989
Natural Sweet Wine
Grown, Made and Bottled on
Klein Constantia, Constantia.
Product of South Africa.
500ml   15,5% vol
A296

Robert Mondavi and Opus One

If there is one name around the world that symbolizes the drive and ambition of California's wine-makers, it is that of Robert Mondavi. Since its foundation in 1966, the Robert Mondavi winery has remained at the forefront of all kinds of research aimed at producing the best wines possible and of understanding the highly complex process of wine-making. Most people would have kept the results of all this research to themselves, but one of the most engaging aspects of Mondavi's character is his constant willingness to share the fruits of his experience, often dearly earned, with those who show an interest. This means that Robert Mondavi has not only developed his own business in a spectacular manner, but has also contributed to wine knowledge in general. His family history symbolizes, in many ways, the American success story. His parents emigrated from Italy and settled initially in Minnesota, then moved to California, where his father started a wine-merchant business. After studying at Stanford University, Robert Mondavi worked with his father at the Charles Krug Winery in Napa Valley, north of San Francisco. In 1966, he started his owns winery, which currently spans over 1,500 acres of vineyards and whose diversified production is remarkably reliable in quality. The company is now partially public, but remains controlled by the family. Over and above this well earned success, Robert Mondavi has taken into consideration that wine does not exist on its own, but is integrated into a way of life. This is shown by many of his company's activities. The Mondavi music festival is one of the richest of the region. The winery is a veritable cultural center, harboring painting and sculpture exhibits, and its buildings are an homage to local Mexican architectural traditions. This building receives over 300,000 visitors each year and is thus one of California's top destinations. It is designed to have something to offer for everyone with an interest in wine, from the novice to the connoisseur.

Behind the wines and the showcase that is given them, there is a strong ecological and aesthetic fiber to current activities at the Mondavi winery. Above all, practical applications are shown for all forms of research. The vast subject of wine education and the association of wine and food are good examples. Clearly Mondavi hasn't forgotten a lesson learned from his mother, an excellent cook, who considered it absurd to select wines for a final blend without testing them first with food. In the case of a substance as complex as wine, the role of education in the creation and development of taste for wine has been fully understood by Mondavi. It was not fortuitous that another man convinced of the interactions between wine and culture, Baron Philippe de Rothschild, decided that Robert Mondavi was the ideal partner for a very innovative project: a joint venture between Bordeaux and Napa Valley to produce a great wine. It was Philippe de Rothschild who suggested the idea to Robert Mondavi in 1970, and the first vintage came in 1979. The futuristic Opus One

Opposite: The main building of the Robert Mondavi Winery uses the style of the Spanish missionaries, who were the first to plant vineyards in California.
Above: The vineyard around the winery, near Yountville in the Napa Valley.

145

winery, purpose-built, was inaugurated in 1991. A visit to this extraordinary building gives the powerful impression that a couple of generations have made centuries' worth of progress here, if only to come back to a few essential truths about the making of fine wine.

From the outset with Opus One, the objective was clear: to make the best possible wine from Napa Valley grapes by combining the know-how of Mouton-Rothschild and Mondavi. This is approaches to wine-making has been achieved by integrating the teams. Patrick Léon, a Frenchman, and Tim Mondavi, an American, share responsibility for wine-making, with a Frenchwoman, Geneviève Jansens, in charge of production, and an American team handling the marketing. Everything has been conceived with this goal in mind: making a great and long-lived wine, using the best characteristics of the Cabernet Sauvignon grape within a blend that uses other Bordeaux varieties.

on the part of the project's fathers, that something was possible. To judge by the reactions of those who visit the Opus One winery, the exceptional quality of the wine stands out. Once again, the educational aspect of the guided tour has been carefully thought out, integrating elements from the two parent cultures. Nowadays, after some years of over-exposure to technology in wineries, Robert Mondavi, like many others, recommends a simpler, more reasonable

remarkably close to the ideas that presided over the creation of the estates which were to become Bordeaux first growths, by men like Pontac and Ségur in the eighteenth century. The enormous advantage that Opus One had was the knowledge acquired since then. Very few wine estates are actually able to concentrate wholly on a single objective. Marrying Californian and Bordeaux It has taken a dozen vintages to begin to reveal the potential of this wine. This has been the time necessary to fine-tune each part of the process, and it is certainly not over, as a great wine needs a lot of time, both to be made and then to be judged. Teamwork on such a project is a key element, but the considerable investments made, in time and money, would all have been to no avail without the initial vision, approach to wine-making. He says that the starting point of any great wine is in the vineyard, and his explanation uses the analogy of food. Bad produce cannot be disguised in the kitchen by clever cooking. A lifetime's experience of fine wines has in no way dulled the communicative enthusiasm of this man, who, at over eighty years old, has the energy of someone twenty years younger.

Opposite: Magnificent trees border the vineyards at the edge of the valley.
Above (upper): A Cabernet Sauvignon vine in flower.
Above (lower): Labeling reflects ecological concerns.

TASTING

In the vast range of wines produced by Mondavi, all are reputed for their regularity. Although Cabernet Sauvignon and Chardonnay constitute the classics, the Sauvignon Blanc shows an interesting and more original tendancy.

◆ *Robert Mondavi*
Cabernet Sauvignon Reserve
This wine is made for aging, as the 1979, which still tastes beautifully, proved.

◆ *1990*
The nose is quite tight to begin with, before opening up on some concentrated fruit aromas and a touch of wood. The mouth feel is supple and luxuriant, with a woody edge, and fine, smooth tannins.

◆ *Sauvignon Blanc, Stag's Leap 1994*
Robert Mondavi has done much to raise awareness of this grape variety in the United States, and he believes that the particular meso-climate of the Stag's Leap district is very much suited to it. This is a good example of the style, with sharp and fresh green fruit aromas. The grape flavors come right through into the glass, and there is an interesting balance between softness and the freshness of the fruit flavors. Delicious.

◆ *Opus One*
Opus One is blended from the three main Bordeaux grape varieties. Cabernet Sauvignon is very much the dominant partner, with proportions that vary between eighty percent and ninety seven percent according to the year. The rest is from Merlot and Cabernet Franc. When tasting the younger vintages, it is worth remembering that it is a wine for keeping. We are just tasting the future.

◆ *1980*
A magnificent nose, still very young and richly expressive. The fresh fruit aromas have changed into jam, with a range of nuances like blackberry, cassis, and cherry. One can feel how the wine has aged gracefully, holding on to a reminder of its youth while acquiring the wisdom of years. On the palate, the impression is smooth, with a firm but gently smoky flavor. The fruit lingers on, and the balance is perfect between suppleness and grip, which lifts the aftertaste. Perfectly ready for drinking now and very good.

Stag's Leap Wine Cellars

In 1880, a few years before writing *Dr. Jekyll and M. Hyde,* the Scottish writer Robert Louis Stevenson got married in San Francisco and decided to spend his honeymoon in Silverado, an abandoned mining camp in the hills above Napa Valley. It was here that Stevenson the traveler and wine-lover took time out to write a few lines in his diary about the birth of wine-making in the region. While doing so, he had before his mind the fact that European vineyards were, at that moment, rapidly disappearing under the onslaughts of the then highly resistant phylloxera beetle. Stevenson, like many of his contemporaries, believed that the famous vineyards of Europe had gone forever. He regretted never having tasted Châteauneuf-du-Pape or Hermitage and that the taste of the great Bordeaux wines was now just a memory! And what of the future? The future, for Stevenson, lay in California and in Australia, and his tasting of some of the wines produced in nineteenth century California convinced him of their potential, even if they had not yet, in his opinion, reached their optimum level. Vineyard plantations had started to take the place of mining in some of the valleys above San Francisco. He considered that both activities shared a prospecting approach: "One corner of land after another is tried with one kind of grape after another. This is a failure; that is better; a third best. So, bit by bit, they grope about for their Clos Vougeot and Lafite. Those lodes and pockets of earth, more precious than the precious ores, that yield inimitable fragrance and soft fire; those virtuous Bonanzas, where the soil has sublimated under sun and stars to something finer, and the wine is bottled poetry: these still lie undiscovered; chaparral conceals, thicket embowers them; the miner chips the rock and wanders farther, and the grizzly muses undisturbed. But there thay bide their hour, awaiting their Columbus; and nature nurses and prepares them. The smack of Californian earth shall linger on the palate of your grandson. "

One hundred years later, Europe's vineyards have been entirely reconstituted: the technique of grafting European varieties onto disease-resistant American rootstock was finally discovered. Meanwhile, California has continued its prospecting activity, in search of the best combinations between soil, climate, and grape variety. Furthermore, in the 1930's, a small number of producers like Beaulieu and Inglenook decided to make wines of the highest possible quality that could stand comparison with the best from Europe, particularly from France.

This process speeded up in 1960, with increased plantings of French grape varieties, particularly cabernet sauvignon, a red variety from Bordeaux, and chardonnay, the white variety from Burgundy. Together with the improved plantings came a whole range of technical improvements in wine-making, introduced by intelligent people who were open-minded and had precise goals. A new kind of wine-maker came to Napa Valley. One of these was Warren Winiarski, a former classics professor at the University of Chicago.

Opposite: Stag's Leap is the name given to these cliffs by an Indian legend.
Above: Giant wind machines keep the air moving to protect the vines from spring frosts in Napa Valley.

In their determination to prove that the best wines of California could be comparable to the best of France, they received considerable and unexpected help from a blind tasting that took place in Paris in 1976, organized by Steven Spurrier, founder of l'Académie du Vin. On this occasion, the 1973 vintage of Stag's Leap Wine Cellars Cabernet Sauvignon, which was just the second vintage made by Warren Winiarski on his new estate, came out as best wine of a list of top Californian and Bordeaux growths made essentially from cabernet sauvignon. Just to complete the demonstration, the chardonnay from Château Montelena took first place in the white wine category!

This tasting had considerable impact in the United States. The results of blind tastings of this type need to be taken with some precaution, and of course some people (including, it must be said, skeptics and bad losers), underlined the limits of the approach. Many French critics took the stand that the Californian wines could be excellent in their youth, but that they would not last well. So, ten years later, Spurrier organized a rematch, this time in New York with the same wines from the same vintages, and the results were remarkably similar. There could now be no doubt: California could definitely produce great wines.

Stag's Leap is a tiny area in the southeast corner of Napa Valley. The Silverado Trail runs right through it, so one can almost imagine Stevenson on his way up there pondering on the potential of this stretch of land. It now has its own appellation, or American Viticultural Area. The name Stag's Leap comes from impressive cliffs that rise up from the valley's edge, where, under an Indian legend, a stag that was being hunted once escaped by leaping the huge canyon from one peak to another.

As for Winiarski, his name seems incredibly predestined, as it means, in Polish, "of wine." Having become passionately interested in wine, he decided to change his lifestyle and came to California in 1964 to become a wine-

Above: Soil being prepared prior to replanting.
Below: The garden next to the winery. Nothing incompatible between beauty and great wines.
Opposite: The wine-lover is always welcome in Napa Valley. The entrance to the tasting room at Stag's Leap Wine cellars.

This is in tune with a calmly thought out and aesthetic approach to wine-making. The buildings at Stag's Leap also clearly show this approach, blending perfectly into the landscape, sheltered under a splendid stand of oak trees on a knoll. Warren Winiarski is not someone who would make snap judgments or give instant recipes for making a great wine. He believes that wine responds, in a way like visual arts, to laws of harmony like the golden rule. This implies that the ideal point of balance is not perfectly symmetrical, but includes an off-center dynamic which is fully harmonious, but creates movement. From this it follows that if a wine's taste is the result of a tension between an impression of fullness on one hand and one of motion on the other, then a great wine must balance the feelings of satisfaction and stimulation. Such a balance is also to be sought after in the vineyard, as Winiarski does not consider that the age of the vine plant is necessarily a crucial factor in the quality of the fruit it produces. This is much more a matter of its equilibrium and general health. The best illustration of this, put into practice, can be given by a walk in his vineyards, which are tended like a garden. Instinct and intellect can come together in wine-making. The story of Stag's Leap wine cellars and the personality of Warren Winiarski, like that of a few others in California, are there to prove it.

maker. In 1968, a taste of a wine made by Nathan Fay, from a vineyard plot in Stag's Leap, convinced him of the potential of this area and, in 1970, he managed to purchase some land right next to the plot of his friend.

Today, the wines from Stag's Leap Wine Cellars are in the top league of Napa Valley classics, and one of them, Cask 23, is about the most expensive wine made in the United States. The most striking thing about Winiarski's wines is their balance.

TASTING

◆ *Cabernet Sauvignon Cask 23*
A magnificent nose, both complex and fine, with delicate touches of flowers and wonderfully fresh fruit. Everything seems to have melted together and become sublimated. The same impression of balance is the dominant sensation on the palate, which is dense but not over-concentrated. The wine is still very young, and the tannins are rounded and solid, but the superb quality of the fruit makes one want to drink it already. The finish is impressively long and fresh. This is surely one of the world's greatest cabernets.

Ridge Vineyards

This is the highest vineyard in California. Planted in the Santa Cruz mountains, barely sixty five miles south of San Francisco, the vineyard culminates at an altitude of 1,965 feet on a ridge called Monte Bello, the beautiful mountain. The Monte Bello vineyard and winery was founded in 1885 by an Italian immigrant called Osae Perrone, who built a cellar with limestone blocks quarried out of the hill. This cellar still exists today, and with its various extensions, it holds a good part of the current production of Ridge Vineyards.

Sheltered from the coastal mists, the Monte Bello vineyard is ideally situated: a mountain range protects it from the sea, and its altitude supplies the cool nighttime temperatures and the gentle daytime breezes that make life so pleasant, both for man and for grapes. What is more, the site is particularly impressive, with a grandiose and spectacular view from the hillcrest which overlooks, just below the vineyard on the seaward side, the San Andreas fault that runs through California. Wine is far from being the main activity of the area however: in the valley below, on the eastern side, lies the world's highest concentration of sophisticated technological industries, which has given it the name of Silicon Valley. The contrast is striking between the peaceful suburban life down in the valley, with its streets lined with quietly attractive houses built of traditional materials, carefully integrated into landscaped gardens, and the still wild nature of the hills above. The bears have long since deserted this area, but driving up to Ridge in the early morning, you may well be startled by the whistle of a hawk's wings as it swoops down on its prey. The ridge which gives its name to the vineyard acts as a divider between two meso-climates, but it is also a dividing edge for light, between two

Above: Cabernet sauvignon vines climb over the hilltop that forms the highest part of the Ridge Monte Bello vineyard.

angles or duration of sunlight, especially when the divider runs north-south, as here. Most of the Monte Bello vineyard, planted on the eastern facing slope, is perfectly sheltered from the Pacific winds. Of the wine estates founded in California in the nineteenth century, few have survived to this day. Not only did phylloxera take its toll, but those who survived this pest were hard put to survive what the politicians had in store for them. Prohibition, between 1919 and 1933, obliged most wine-makers interested in producing fine wine to abandon their estates. This explains why the history of most of the best-known wineries in California is so recent. Ridge is a typical example of the new deal in American wine-making. It all started nearby, at Stanford University, famous for its research departments. In 1959, three engineers from Stanford, who had become interested in wine during their spare time, decided to buy the former vineyard of Perrone and thus created Ridge Vineyards. They gradually

Above: Part of the buildings at Ridge Vineyards, this fine wooden barn is surrounded by a garden and backed onto the hill.

improved and enlarged it, and, in 1969 a philosophy graduate from Stanford named Paul Draper joined them. Paul Draper was a wine-lover before becoming a wine-maker, which is probably a key point in the development of the specific style of Ridge, as Draper makes wine above all to suit his palate rather than according to technical norms. Even today, his considerable experience has not transformed Paul Draper into a man full of theories, but he is visibly one of the most thoughtful wine-makers in the world. It is fair to say that Draper, through considerable observation and an insistence on a less interventionist approach to wine-making, is probably the most significant contributor to the renaissance of what might be called a typically Californian style of wine. Zinfandel is a grape variety practically unknown outside California, where it is the most widely planted grape, used to make all kinds of wine. Nobody seems to know where it originated, but its adaptability to the local climates and its

capacity to produce all types of wine made it a favorite with the early vineyard pioneers. Paul Draper managed to localize some of the old vineyard plots dating from before Prohibition days. For years, he just bought their grapes and made the wine, but Ridge Vineyards has recently purchased two of the best plots in the Sonoma Valley. For anyone who wants to taste something really different, with heady aromas like a bouquet straight out of the Arabian Nights, Ridge's two wines named after their Sonoma vineyards, Geyserville and Lytton Springs, are a must. The intensity of the sensations that these wines give surely has a link with the presence of vines over a hundred years old in these vineyards. Paul Draper's opinion is that the wine-maker is more a midwife to a wine than a creator. The same soft approach goes for the vineyard "terroir," that unique combination of soil and meso-climate that gives grapes from one plot a unique flavor. The nature of fruit has to be respected at all stages, in order to give each wine its specific characteristics. Because it is the individual vineyards that make the difference, Ridge places their names in large letters on its labels, following the approach of most great European wines, in a country which has recently been obsessed with the name of the grape variety.

TASTING

◆ *Monte Bello 1991*
The nose is rich and heady, with deep aromas of eucalyptus, which emerge from an apparent austerity. The palate is full-flavored and ample, with lots of freshness. The smooth elegant texture goes with strong fruit flavors that last through to a long finish. These sensations went perfectly with the dishes served on the occasion. Certainly a great wine.

◆ *Lytton Springs 1991*
Made with eighty percent Zinfandel, blended with some Carignan, Petite Sirah, and Grenache, this is a monster of a wine! A fabulous concentration of fruit and spices comes to the nose, only to be confirmed on the palate. The feeling is both soft and explosive. Sheer pleasure. What is amazing in such a powerful wine is the absence of any trace of harshness.

Inniskillin Icewine

Just imagine the Great North and its vast open spaces blanketed by snow for much of the year. Coming south a way, to the border between Canada and the United States, you find the most impressive waterfalls in the world: Niagara Falls. All this adds up to a strange sensation that mingles a thrilling form of chill with a dose of vertigo, in any case something far distant from the usual visions that are conjured up by the idea of wine country. But in fact, it is precisely the combination between these two elements— great cold and a huge mass of water—that enable the production of one of the world's most unusual wines.

In the case of the finest wines, it is the interaction between their production and the place in which they are produced that endows them, whatever the size of the vineyard, with the characteristics that render each wine so unique. The geographical situation of Canada is far from producing, in most people's minds, images of vineyards, so it comes as a surprise to many to discover that the latitude of the Niagara Falls area is about the same as that of Châteauneuf-du-Pape in southern France. But climate is not simply determined by the distance that separates a given place from the poles of this earth. This Great Lakes region, which crosses the border between Canada and the United States, has a particular meso-climate that enables it to produce wine despite winters which often last for more than half the year. In coastal wine regions, such as California or Bordeaux, the nearby oceans

Opposite: The Inniskillin estate is close to the Niagara River, ten miles or so downstream from the famous waterfalls.
Above: The estate buildings were inspired by the great American architect Frank Lloyd Wright.

oceans moderate the climate; in this case, the role of the vast mass of water formed by lakes Erie and Ontario is even more critical. Extremes of heat in the summer and of cold in the winter are considerably attenuated. It is a particular combination of sufficient warmth at the end of the ripening season and cold winters that set in early which has enabled the production of the region's most singular wine, suitably called Icewine. The technique of making sweet wines from very ripe grapes that have literally been frozen on the vines originated in certain vineyards in Germany and Austria, where these wines are called Eiswein. Usually made from the Riesling grape, the Eisweins from the Mosel and Rhine valleys are benchmarks of the style, and their quality, longevity, and scarcity places them as the world's most expensive wines. At Inniskillin, the grape variety used to make Icewine is a hybrid called Vidal, so it could be said that this is a unique case of hybrids producing one of the world's greatest wines. Thanks to the suitability of its climate, Ontario, and in particular the region of Niagara Falls, has become the world's largest producer of this type of wine.

By coincidence (or is it really such a coincidence?), one of the founders of Inniskillin, Karl Kaiser, comes from Austria. In any case, Inniskillin's Icewine has rapidly become the pride of Canada, winning a Grand Prix d'Honneur at the 1991 edition of Vinexpo, the world's biggest wine exhibition, which is held every two years in Bordeaux.

To make an Icewine, the grapes must remain on the vine long after the fall of the leaves and right into the heart of winter, in December or January. These ripe grapes are alternately frozen and then thawed out, producing a gradual dehydration effect. All the natural ingredients in the grape—sugars, acids, and solid matter—are thereby concentrated to an essence. This means that each plant will only be capable of producing between five and ten percent of the normal quantity of juice when the

grapes are finally crushed. Grapes are therefore so precious that great care is taken to protect them from birds by all manner of netting, right up to harvest time. Harvesting is generally done in the very early morning, when it is still dark, to make sure that the grapes are still frozen when they reach the pressing room. Picking grapes at -10° C (-50° F) is difficult work, but there are so many volunteers at Inniskillin that you have to book a place two years ahead! After the pressing, the rare drops that flow will take many months to ferment and will finally

Opposite (upper): Frozen grapes are picked in the early morning when the temperature drops to -10°C. Above: The precious grapes are protected from birds by netting. Opposite (below): Part of the vineyard. Below: The lighthouse at Niagara.

produce a wine not very rich in alcohol, but exceptionally concentrated in aromas and flavors.

TASTING

◆ *Inniskillin Icewine 1989*
The magnificent color of this wine is almost impossible to define. It hovers around tinges of old gold, amber, and orange, and literally glows and shines. The nose is very intense and instantly pleasurable, giving off successive layers of aromas that seem to grow out of the glass as a contact is built up between the wine and the air. Flowers, vegetables, crystalized fruit, and tobacco are part of the scene, and everything seems deeply roasted and yet perfectly fresh. The same contrast strikes the palate, where fruit flavors are initially carried by a powerfully austere acidity, which gradually blends with the rich sugar content to show the full

range of aromas found on the nose. These flavors are both of fresh and dried fruit. They linger and seem to cling to the palate, turning to marmalade and finally to coffee and caramel.

Words simply fall short to describe such a complex range of flavors. The only solution

Penfold's Grange

The history of wine in Australia is almost as old as that of California. About the same time as Franciscan monks planted vines in what was later to become a state of the United States and its largest wine producer, the first Governor of the young British colony of Australia imported plants from the Cape. Watching these young plants grow in 1788, Captain Arthur Philip had these prophetic words: "With such a favorable climate, viticulture can reach a state of perfection here, and, if no other form of commerce distracts the colonists, the wines of New South Wales could well become eagerly sought after and irreplaceable on the tables of Europe." It was to take two hundred years for his prophecy for Australia's wines to come true. Today, Australia is one of the rare wine-producing countries to be greatly increasing the acreage of its vineyards, and has, over the past twenty years or so, sped up a movement towards the production of quality wines. The undoubtedly dynamic nature of Australian viticulture is rooted in two cultures that manage to cohabit. On the one hand, just four companies control ninety percent of Australian wine production, while on the other, a large number of small and independently-minded producers are particularly creative and empowered by the pioneering spirit. This does not mean that creativity in wine-making cannot exist within the larger companies, as the story of Grange illustrates perfectly. However, it can be a struggle for survival against shortsighted reasoning from the "bottom-line men," as Max Shubert, the creator of Grange, was to discover. Australia's now flourishing fine wine world owes a statue to this man. Having worked for Penfolds since 1931, he finally managed

Above: The Penfolds winery where Grange is made may not be beautiful, but it produces some great wine! Opposite: Max Shubert, the man who started it all.

to travel to Europe for the first time in 1950 to study European vineyards. When staying in Bordeaux with Christian Cruse, he was given the opportunity to taste older wines that had retained wonderful smells and taste. This was a revelation of the aging potential of wines to Max Shubert, and he decided to do what he could to improve the quality of Australian wines, which were, at the time, simply mediocre. He was determined that the wine he had in mind should have true Australian character, so he picked on the Shiraz grape, which is the Australian name for the Syrah that produces the great wines from the northern Rhône valley: wines like Côte Rôtie and Hermitage. He started making this wine almost in secrecy within the Penfolds winery, giving it the name of "Bin 95."

Above: The Syrah grape is called Shiraz in Australia. Dry climate imposes wide spacing between the rows of vines.

ᵗᵗtion usually stirs controversy, and
the initial reaction of the company
management was not what he had hoped
for. In fact, he was ordered to stop making
the wine! Fortunately for the wine world,
though, Shubert was a determined
man, and he managed to continue his
experiments in secret. When the tide
finally turned, he decided to call the wine
Grange Hermitage, after the farm of the
founder of Penfolds, Grange Farm, and in
homage to one of the prime vineyards for
the Syrah grape in France. Grange had
shown that Shubert was right in his initial
inspiration, namely that great wines
require time to reveal their full potential.
The fact that its taste was radically
different from what the first tasters had
been used to also explains, to a large
extent, why it was at first rejected. Since
then, Grange has established itself as the
most desirable of Australian wines, and
many have followed its example in terms
of wine-making.

Unusually for one of the world's greatest
wines, the grapes for Grange do not
always come from the same vineyard. The
idea is a selection of the best possible fruit,
within the standards of an established
style. Naturally, there is a basis of
vineyard plots that ensures a continuity of
this style, but the emphasis is placed on
fruit selection rather then grape origin.
This approach, together with superb
wine-making, has enabled Grange to
achieve regularity at a high level over the
past forty years: assuredly the hallmark
of a great wine.

Grange's style is unique, and rides out
fashion as do other wines of strong
personality, from Europe or elsewhere.
The birth of a great wine is due to a blend
of natural potential, inspiration, and
strong purpose. Max Shubert, who
provided two-thirds of this blend, rightly
has the final word: "I hope that Grange,
and the welcome it has received as a fine
wine from Australia, has shown that we
are capable of producing wines that equal
the world's best. But we must continue to
be imaginative and act on the strength of
our convictions."

TASTING

♦ *Grange 1990*
*The nose is tightly bound and intense, with
deep black fruit aromas together with
something smoky, like tar. The overall
impression is both airy and firmly anchored
with both feet on the ground. The flavors
literally explode on the palate, smoky and
minty with a spicy edge which livens up the
finish. It's all in there, still very young, but
ready to go and already giving great pleasure.
A great wine that will age for decades.*

Cloudy Bay

The history of wine-making in New Zealand is not one of the longest, and, to be truthful, it was not very glorious until the 1980's. In fact, during the years after the Second World War, an official international commission went so far as to affirm that most of the local production was unfit for human consumption, at least in other countries than New Zealand! Did they not consider New Zealanders as human beings? Progress in terms of wine is closely linked to exchange, and New Zealand was isolated from the rest of the world for so long that this resulted in a lack of wine culture. It was not until 1979 that the first wine bar opened in the country, for example. Since than, things have moved at a spectacular pace, and New Zealand's production of white wine, particularly from the Sauvignon Blanc grape, has become world-renowned.

Cloudy Bay, whose name and label are so evocative of cool, far-away flavors, perfectly illustrates both the speed of this rise to fame and the specific characteristics of many of New Zealand's white wines. The 1985 vintage was made almost in the back of a truck, and this, its first wine, became an overnight success. Ten years later, the Cloudy Bay winery produces ten thousand cases of the most sought-after Sauvignon Blanc in the world. It is a wine whose success is largely due to the specific and very explosive flavors of its fruit. In this instance, as elsewhere in the wine world, an essential part is played by the local soil-climate combination, that of the Wairau Valley in the county of Marlborough, on New Zealand's South Island. New Zealand, following other countries, has begun the process of identifying and defining specific areas that are favorable to fine wine

Above: The sign that marks the entrance to the Cloudy Bay estate.
Above and opposite: Those hazy mountain silhouettes on the label were not just invented by a smart draftsman.
Right: This is the land that produces one of the world's most sought-after Sauvignon Blancs.

◆ Cloudy Bay Sauvignon Blanc 1995
The color is pale, of a whitish gold tone
with a greenish tinge. The nose takes one
on a journey through an orchard planted
with all kinds of fruit: gooseberries, kiwi,
mango, and apple, all very fresh and lively.
Similar flavors come through on the palate,
with a touch of roundness that makes them
instantly seductive. The balance is not one
of complexity, but perfectly delicious.

name. The valley is sheltered from the wind and the rain that drive in from the ocean to the west by a range of mountains. Abundant rainfall on this side is evident from the green-clad slopes, whereas, just across the valley, another range of mountains lies dry and parched. Cool climate and a large number of sunshine hours during the crucial ripening period contribute to the quality of Marlborough's wines. In fact, there is a local Maori saying that claims the sun always shines on Wairau Valley. Just a glimpse at these mountain ranges through the plane 's windows gives the impression of looking at a label of Cloudy Bay. The name comes from the bay into which the Wairau River flows. Originally named by Captain Cook, who anchored here after a difficult passage through the straits that bear his name, it signifies the muddiness of the waters in the bay after storms had increased the flow of water from the Wairau Valley. Although this story may provide somewhat less romantic imagery than the name on its own, it is certain that the combination of name and label, which truly reflect the magic of the place, have contributed to the wine's success.

Once again, in the creation of a wine that is on its way to becoming a modern classic, intuitive genius played a key part. David Hohnen had already founded an excellent winery in Western Australia, called Cape Mentelle, when he had the idea of Cloudy Bay and hired Kevin Judd to run the winery. Of the wines in Cloudy Bay's range, it is its initial wine, Sauvignon Blanc, which has stuck in the minds of amateurs the world around. This surely has to do with fruit flavors of exceptional intensity that are fresh without revealing the kind of acidity that cleans one's teeth in a second. Despite harvest conditions that can be, to put things mildly, unpredictable, Cloudy Bay has never ceased, since its inception, to be an example to follow for New Zealand wines. And many have followed. This is one of the hallmarks of a great wine: to have started a movement, over and above a trend.

production. Marlborough will be one of them.

To reach Cloudy Bay, coming from New Zealand's capital, Wellington, you have to cross the Cook Straits, and the easiest way is to take the small plane, locally known as the "flying pencil." Although very short, the ride can be rough, as the mountainous nature of the terrain generates frequent air turbulence. Flying over Wairau Valley gives one a rapid insight into some of the key points to the success of Cloudy Bay: climate, label, and

PRACTICAL GUIDE

If you wish to visit the regions or even the individual wineries that appear in this book, this section includes a few words of advice, based on past experience and that acquired while researching for this book. You will find, further on, the full addresses for each winery.

General advice

Each country, and in many cases each wine-producing region, has its own traditions regarding what one can describe as "wine tourism." Thankfully for us visitors, these traditions evolve, generally for the better, and infrastructures designed to inform and help the tourist are increasing in the main areas. All the areas mentioned in this book have their individual style, as regards landscape, architecture, and so on, and all of them, at most times of the year, are either spectacularly or quietly beautiful. The best single piece of advice, anywhere in the world, is to telephone ahead for an appointment if you want to visit a specific estate. Most of those in this book will welcome your visit, but there may be a few exceptions.

In all events, avoid trying to visit during harvest time, except for the bigger estates, which are equipped to handle two very different activities at one time. Harvest time in the northern hemisphere is anywhere between late August and mid-October, and between the end of March and mid-May in the southern hemisphere. You must bear in mind that wineries have to produce in order to sell, and they only get one chance a year to do the former, so all energies tend to be mobilized to make the harvest, and the ensuing wine-making, a success. Those who have public relations staff will usually be able to accommodate you, and it is certainly worth living the heady experience of grape harvest once, for the sometimes bacchanalian relief that pickers show after a hard day's work, when the roads become slippery with fresh grape juice, and for the sight and smell of the grapes as they are pressed.

THE NEW WORLD AND THE OLD WORLD

What are referred to as "New World" countries, in terms of wine-making, are the African, American and Oceanic areas. In terms of the contents of this book, that means South Africa, California, Canada, Australia and New Zealand, and it has to be said that these countries are often far better organized, in terms of wine tourism, than those of the "Old World," in other words Europe. This is easily understandable, as the development of a taste for wine, in countries where this has not been an intrinsic part of culture for centuries, can only come through a constant educational effort that includes welcoming tourists, whereas in most European countries, wine has been produced for over a thousand years, and has gradually become an inherent part of the cultural environment. This has the unfortunate disadvantage of leading many people, including producers, to take several things for granted, and consequently neglect the educational and commercial role played by properly welcoming visitors. In a competitive world market, this is thankfully changing rapidly. In New World countries, and in the lesser-known wine regions of Europe, a considerable part of business for smaller wineries derives from cellar-door sales, which give them their generic title of "boutique wineries."

FRANCE

Wine tourism in France has made considerable progress in recent years, although many improvements should be made. Both heritage and depth are considerable that potential is huge. Thankfully, efforts have been made in many parts of France over recent years to make visitors feel welcome. Burgundy and Alsace are a real joy to visit, and the reception for a wine-lover can be quite extraordinary. Learning to be patient in order to acquire a few bottles of the rarest and most sought-after wines is a part of the game that should be learned in Burgundy, if one's aim is to visit some of the top names who produce tiny quantities from single vineyards. There definitely is something in that old saying that goes something like this: the Burgundians have nothing to sell, but will give you a taste of everything in their cellar, whereas the Bordelais have apparently huge stocks but you can consider yourself lucky if you get to taste a single wine. This is, sadly, particularly true of some of the most famous estates, whether this be the ransom for glory or an attitude that seems supercilious towards true amateurs. Bordeaux can, and should, improve in this field.

In Champagne, most of the big houses do a good job of informing the visitor, although some of the visits have a distinctly commercial accent to them. Choose a house that only accepts visits with a rendez vous and in small groups, as this should give you a more individual welcome. The hostesses usually speak several languages, and the visit to the underground cellars of one of the great houses in Reims or elsewhere can be a magical moment. Alsace is one of France's paradises for tourism, and wines and gastronomy play a major part in this. As in the less well organized but fascinating areas of the Loire Valley, the Côtes du Rhône, or the extensive stretch from Provence to Languedoc-Roussillon (which collectively has the potential to become France's California), always make an appointment to visit a particular winery.

ITALY

Italy produces more wines than any other country in the world. This is not a recent phenomenon, as the Ancient Greeks named the peninsula "Oenotria" (the land of wine).

The two wine-producing regions mentioned in this book, the Langhe hills in Piedmont and the western part of Tuscany, are extremely beautiful and leaving them behind is usually heart-rending. Vines climb over the Langhe hills, and the twin denominations of Barolo and Barbaresco are full of treasures. It is worth bearing in mind that most estates are small, and that the owner, fortunately for the quality of his wine, spends much time in his vineyard. Around the township of Bolgheri, vines are not such a dominant part of the scene as in the central part of Tuscany, between Florence and Siena, which is the home of Chianti. But the sea is close, and there are wonderful spots in the small fishing ports, like the Gambero Rosso restaurant.

SPAIN AND PORTUGAL

The two areas mentioned in this book are quite close together, although the vineyards of Spain, in particular, are vastly extensive. The Douro Valley, from which port wine originates, is one of the world's most spectacular vineyard areas. You should begin or end your visit in Villa Nova da Gaia, a suburb of Oporto, where nearly all port is aged before shipping, and where the houses have their headquarters.

GERMANY

The Mosel Valley, with its twin tributaries the Saar and the Ruwer, is one of the world's most spectacularly beautiful vineyard sites. The town of Trier was a major Roman town, and the vineyards spread out along the river banks on steep hillside slopes. Cruising down the valley, whether by boat or on land, is a pleasure for the eyes and a permanent invitation to taste the wonderfully delicate white wines that are the glory of the German tradition. The small towns, such as Bernkastel, are neat as a pin, and information for visitors easy to find.

Further to the north, the Mosel flows into the Rhine and the valley widens out. Being nearer to large cities, there are all kinds of industrial activities and larger numbers of tourists here. A series of fine old small towns, with long wine-making traditions, are marvelous to visit, and producers, on the whole, welcome visitors, but it is always best to telephone ahead.

AUSTRIA

Austria certainly counts as one of the European countries where progress in wine-making and in the way wine tourists are informed has been the most spectacular over recent years. The wine museum in the lovely small town of Rust is exemplary, but Styria, to the south, is also worth visiting.

HUNGARY

One of the fastest moving of the former Eastern Bloc communist countries, a visit to Hungary will surprise you. Do not expect everything to function perfectly, but the Tokay area, near the eastern extremity of the country, will give you a feel for Central Europe and its rich tradition of extraordinary sweet white wines.

NORTH AMERICA

California, and the Napa Valley in particular, is a veritable paradise for anyone who wishes to travel around a wine theme. Everything is done to inform and guide the visitor, to supply him with all manners of distractions, more or less linked to wine and the local history, in an area which is naturally beautiful. The small but growing wine industry in Canada follows a similar approach.

AUSTRALIA, NEW ZEALAND AND SOUTH AFRICA

Wine-growing areas frequently set in spectacular landscapes, uncrowded and unpolluted environments, and welcoming wineries are the rule here. There is a clear awareness, on the part of those in charge of the wineries, that the visitor may have come half-way around the world to visit their promised land.

How to travel to the world's great wine countrie

To reach most of the countries that produce the wines that appear in this book, it is practically essential to take a plane. In this case, the first contact with a country is often the welcome you receive on board the flag-flying company of the country concerned. In our travels for researching and taking the photographs for this book, we tried a number of these companies, bearing in mind the attitude and pre-occupations of a wine-lover. Here are the results:

GERMANY: Lufthansa

Lufthansa has easily the best flight network leading into Germany. The service is courteous and efficient, and the staff highly competent. As with most companies, the wine selection is very limited in tourist or economy class, but you will find up to half a dozen German wines on the wine list in Business and First Class. The presentation is particularly good in First Class, with an illustrated booklet in four languages that gives information on each wine.

AUSTRIA: Lauda Air

We particularly appreciated the style and the quality of service on board of this small company. Although the planes which link Paris to Vienna (the line we tried), are small, the service is perfect and worthy of many company's long-distance business class. One does not find many companies whose stewardesses can recite their wines lists on every type of flight by memory! Whatever class you fly, the food is served in porcelain, and the serviettes are cloth, rather than paper. The wine selection is short, but well chosen, although there is more choice on longer flights. Austrian wines are to the forefront, which is just as well, as this country drinks 90 percent of its production, so it is difficult to get to know Austrian wine elsewhere.

HUNGARY: Malev

The Hungarian national company is called Malev, and it has financial ties with Alitalia. Exclusively Hungarian wines are served on all flights, and these are identifiable by the names of the grape varieties. The long distance flights, in particular, feature the excellent red wines from the Villanyi region, in the south of Hungary. Shorter flights serve wines from those sad little quarter bottles.

USA: American Airlines

Although not a national company, American Airlines proudly bears the name of the continent that was taken from the first name of the explorer Amerigo Vespucci. Its network between the United States and Europe is one of the largest, especially now that it operates a link with British Airways. The wine lists in Business Class and First Class are classic in their conception, and evenly balanced between French and Californian wines. An originality is the availability of a good vintage port by the glass. The wines are presented in a fairly basic booklet, but a video guide provides useful additional information.

Addresses

LEBANON, THE BEKAA PLAIN
CHÂTEAU MUSAR
BP 281 - Imm Sopenco
Rue Baroudy Achrafleh
Beirut - LEBANON
TEL: 961 1 201 928 - FAX: 961 1 201 827

FRANCE, BORDEAUX
CHÂTEAU MARGAUX
33460 Margaux
TEL: 33 05 57 88 70 28 - FAX: 33 05 57 88 31 32

CHÂTEAU LATOUR
33250 Pauillac
TEL: 33 05 56 73 19 80 - FAX: 33 05 56 73 19 81

CHÂTEAU LAFITE-ROTHSCHILD
33250 Pauillac
TEL: 33 05 56 73 18 18 - FAX: 33 05 56 59 26 83

CHÂTEAU MOUTON-ROTHSCHILD
10, rue de Grassi - 33250 Pauillac
TEL: 33 05 56 73 20 20 - FAX: 33 05 56 73 20 44

CHÂTEAU HAUT-BRION
133, avenue Jean Jaurès - BP 24
33602 Pessac cedex
TEL: 33 05 56 00 29 30 - FAX: 33 05 56 98 75 14

PÉTRUS
Établissements Jean-Pierre Moueix - BP 129
33502 Libourne
TEL: 33 05 57 51 93 66 - FAX: 33 05 57 51 79 79

CHÂTEAU CHEVAL BLANC
33330 Saint-Émilion
TEL: 33 05 57 55 55 55 - FAX: 33 05 57 55 55 50

CHÂTEAU D'YQUEM
Sauternes - 33210 Langon
TEL: 33 05 57 98 07 07 - FAX: 33 05 57 98 07 08

FRANCE, CHAMPAGNE
BOLLINGER
16, rue Jules-Lobet - 51 160 Ay
TEL: 33 03 26 53 33 66 - FAX: 33 03 26 54 85 59

ROEDERER
21, boulevard Lundy - 51100 Reims
TEL: 33 03 26 40 42 11 - FAX: 33 03 26 47 66 51

KRUG
5, rue Coquebert - 51100 Reims
TEL: 33 03 26 84 44 20 - FAX: 33 03 26 84 44 49

VEUVE CLICQUOT
12, rue du Temple - 51100 Reims
TEL: 33 03 26 89 54 40 - FAX: 33 03 26 40 60 17

FRANCE, BURGUNDY
LA ROMANÉE (voir Bouchard Père et Fils)
Domaine de la Romanée-Conti - 1, rue Derrière-le-Four - 21700 Vosne-Romanée
TEL: 33 03 80 61 04 57 - FAX: 33 03 80 61 05 72

BOUCHARD PÈRE ET FILS
Au château - BP 70 - 21202 Beaune
TEL: 33 03 80 24 80 24 - FAX: 33 03 80 24 97 56

FRANCE, ALSACE
DOMAINE WEINBACH
Clos des Capucins - 25, route du Vin
68240 Kaysersberg
TEL: 33 03 89 47 13 21 - FAX: 33 03 89 47 38 18

ZIND-HUMBRECHT
4, rue de Colmar - BP 22 - 68230 Turckheim
TEL: 33 03 89 27 02 05 - FAX: 33 03 89 27 22 58

FRANCE, JURA
CHÂTEAU D'ARLAY
39140 Arlay
TEL: 33 04 84 85 04 22 - FAX: 33 04 84 48 17 96

FRANCE, CÔTES-DU-RHÔNE
CHÂTEAU-GRILLET
42410 Vérin
TEL: 33 04 74 59 51 56 - FAX: 33 04 78 92 96 10

É. GUIGAL
69420 Ampuis
TEL: 33 04 74 56 10 22 - FAX: 33 04 74 56 18 76

CHÂTEAU DE BEAUCASTEL
Chemin de Beaucastel - 84350 Courthezon
TEL: 33 04 90 70 41 00 - FAX: 33 04 90 70 41 19

FRANCE, LANGUEDOC
MAS DE DAUMAS GASSAC
34150 Aniane
TEL: 33 04 67 57 71 28 - FAX: 33 04 67 57 41 03

FRANCE, LOIRE
DOMAINE HUET
11/13, rue de la Croix Buisée - 37210 Vouvray
TEL: 33 02 47 52 78 87 - FAX: 33 02 47 52 66 51

COULÉE DE SERRANT
Château de la Roche aux Moines
49170 Savennières
TEL: 33 02 41 72 22 32 - FAX: 33 02 41 72 28 68

ITALY, TUSCANY
SASSICAIA
Tenuta san guido - 57020 Bolgheri
TEL: 39 56 57 60 17 - FAX: 39 56 57 62 003

ITALY, PIEDMONT
BRUNO GIACOSA
12 057 Neive
TEL: 39 17 36 70 27 - FAX: 39 17 36 77 477

GAJA
Via Torino 36 - 12050 Barbaresco
TEL and FAX: 39 17 36 35 158

SPAIN, CASTILLE-LEÓN
BODEGAS VEGA-SICILIA
E-47259 Valbuena del Duero
TEL: 34 83 68 01 47 - FAX: 34 83 68 02 63

PORTUGAL, PORTO
Taylor Fladgate & Yeatman vinhos S.A.
P.O. Box 1311 - 4401 Vila Nova de Gaia - Codex
TEL: 351 2 37 19 999 - FAX: 351 2 37 08 607

QUINTA DO NOVAL
P.O. Box 57 - 4401 Vila Nova de Gaia
TEL: 351 2 30 20 20 - FAX: 351 2 30 03 65

GERMANY, MOSEL-SAAR-RUWER
WEINGUT J.J. PRÜM
54470 Bernkastel/Wehlen
TEL: 49 65 31 30 91 - FAX: 49 65 31 60 71

MAXIMIN GRÜNHAUS
C. von Schubert'sche
Gutsverwaltung - 54318 Grünhaus/Trier
TEL: 49 65 15 111 - FAX: 49 65 15 212

GERMANY, RHEINGAU
SCHLOSS JOHANNISBERG
65366 Geisenheim/Johannisberg
TEL: 49 67 22 70 09 - FAX: 49 67 22 80 27

WEINGUT ROBERT WEIL
Mühlberg 5 - 65399 Kiedrich/Rheingau
TEL: 49 61 23 23 08 - FAX: 49 61 23 15 46

HUNGARY, TOKAY
TOKAY RENAISSANCE
3910 Tokay - PF 17 - Kossuth ter 15
TEL: 36 47 352 009 - FAX: 36 47 352 141

AUSTRIA, BURGENLAND
RÜSTER AUSBRUCH
Robert Wenzel Weinbau
Hauptstrasse 29 - A 7071 Rust
TEL: 43 02 685 287

SOUTH AFRICA, CAPE PROVINCE
KLEIN CONSTANTIA
P.O. Box 375 - Constantia 7848
TEL: 27 21 79 45 188 - FAX: 27 21 79 42 464

UNITED STATES, NAPA VALLEY
ROBERT MONDAVI - OPUS ONE
P.O. Box 106 - Oakville - California 94 562
TEL: 1 707 963 40 33 and 1 707 963 19 79
FAX: 1 707 963 10 07 and 1 707 944 94 42

STAG'S LEAP WINE CELLARS
5766 Silverado trail - Napa - California 94558
TEL: 1 707 944 20 20 - FAX: 1 707 257 75 01

UNITED STATES, SANTA CRUZ MOUNTAINS
RIDGE VINEYARDS
P.O. Box 1810 - Cuppertino - CA 95015
TEL: 1 408 867 32 44 - FAX: 1 408 867 29 86

CANADA, NIAGARA PENINSULA
INNISKILLIN ICEWINE
RR# 1 - Niagara-on-the-Lake
Ontario - LOS 1J0
TEL: 1 905 468 21 87 - FAX: 1 905 468 53 55

AUSTRALIA
PENFOLD'S GRANGE
Southcorp Wines
PTY limited - Tanunda road - P.O. Box 21
Nuriootpa - S A 5355
TEL: 61 08 56 09 389 - FAX: 61 08 56 09 295

NEW ZEALAND, MARLBOROUGH
CLOUDY BAY
P.O. Box 376 - Blenheim
TEL: 64 3 572 89 11 - FAX: 64 3 572 80 65

Where to find the world's greatest wines in the United States

This list is selective, but not exhaustive. It is not a complete guide of the best wine stores in the country, but aims to give the reader a few addresses which regularly stock many of the wines in this book. Some of the rarer wines may take a little more hunting out, but any good wine store should help you with additional information on where to find a particular wine.

NEW YORK AREA
Sherry-Lehmann, 679 Madison Avenue, New York, NY. Tel: 212 838 7500
Pop's Wines and Spirits, 256 Long Beach Road, Island Park, NY. Tel: 516 431 0025
Zachys Wine and Liquor, 16 East Parkway, Scarsdale, NY. Tel: 914 723 0241

BOSTON AREA
Martignetti's Liquor, 1650 Soldier's Field Road, Brighton, MA. Tel: 617 782 3700
The Wine and Cheese Cask, 407 Washington Street, Somerville, MA. Tel: 617 623 8656
Big Y Wines, 150 North King Street, Northampton, MA. Tel: 413 584 7775

WASHINGTON DC AREA
Calvert Woodley Wine and Liquour, 4339 Connecticut Avenue NW, Washington DC. Tel: 202 966 4400
Mills, 87 Main Street, Annapolis, MD. Tel: 410 263 2888
Total Beverage, 13055C Lee Jackson Highway, Chantilly, VA. Tel: 703 817 1177

CHICAGO AREA
Knightsbridge Wine Shop, 405 Lake Cook Road, Deerfield, IL. Tel: 847 498 4114
Sam's Wine & Spirits, 1720 North Marcey Street, Chicago, IL. Tel: 800 777 9137

MIAMI AREA

Crown Wine Merchants, 6731 Red Road, Coral Gables, FL. Tel: 305 669 0225
Foremost Sunset Corners, 8701 Sunset Drive, Miami, FL. Tel: 305 271 8492
Wine Watch, 901 Progress Drive, Fort Lauderdale, FL. Tel: 954 523 9463

DENVER AREA
The Vineyard, 261 Filmore Street, Denver, CO. Tel: 303 355 8824
Liquor Mart, 1750 15th Street, Boulder, CO. Tel: 303 449 3374

SAN FRANCISCO AREA
Kermit Lynch, 1605 San Pablo Avenue, Berkeley, CA. Tel: 510 524 1524
K&L Wine Merchant, 768 Harrison Street, San Francisco, CA. Tel: 415 896 1734
Wine Club San Francisco, 953 Harrison Street, San Francisco, CA. Tel: 415 512 9086

LOS ANGELES AREA
Hi-Time Cellars, 250 Ogle Street, Costa Mesa, CA. Tel: 714 650 8463
Wine Club Santa Ana, 2110 East McFadden, Santa Ana, CA. Tel: 714 835 6485
The Wine House, 2311 Cotner Avenue, Los Angeles, CA. Tel: 800 626 WINE
Wine Exchange, 2368 North Orange Mall, Orange, CA. Tel: 714 974 1454

SEATTLE AREA
McCarthy & Schiering Wine Merchants, 6500 Ravenne NE, Seattle 98115, WA. Tel: 206 524 9500
Pete's Supermarket, 58 Rast Lynn, Seattle, WA. Tel: 206 322 2660